W9-AYL-243

Get to the Point!

Get to the Point!

Painless Advice for Writing Memos, Letters, and E-mails Your Colleagues and Clients Will Understand

ELIZABETH DANZIGER

 THREE RIVERS PRESS
NEW YORK

Copyright © 2001 by Elizabeth Danziger

All rights reserved. No part of this book may be reproduced or transmitted in any form or by any means, electronic or mechanical, including photo-copying, recording, or by any information storage and retrieval system, without permission in writing from the publisher.

Published by Three Rivers Press, New York, New York.
Member of the Crown Publishing Group.

Random House, Inc. New York, Toronto, London, Sydney, Auckland
www.randomhouse.com

THREE RIVERS PRESS and the Tugboat design are registered trademarks of Random House, Inc.

Printed in the United States of America

Design by Robert Bull Design

Library of Congress Cataloging-in-Publication Data
Danziger, Elizabeth.
    Get to the point : painless advice for writing memos, letters and
  E-mails your colleagues and clients will understand / Elizabeth Danziger.
  Includes bibliographical references.
  (pbk.)
    1. Business writing.   2. Business communication.   3. Commercial
  correspondence.   4. Memorandums.   5. Electronic mail messages.
  6. English language—Business English.   7. English language—
  Rhetoric.   8. English language—Grammar.   I. Title.
HF5718.3 .D36 2001
808'.066665—dc21   2001042726

ISBN 0-609-80760-9

10   9   8   7   6   5   4   3   2   1

First Edition

To my children, Michael, Lily, Ariella, and Sarah,
without whom there would be no point.

Acknowledgments

Many people helped make it possible for me to write this book; a few of them deserve special mention here.

Alan Danziger, my husband, best friend, wisest critic, and the most wonderful father to our children, contributed his calm rationality to the challenging process of writing *Get to the Point*. His unswerving willingness to be available for our children while I was working made it possible for our family to proceed without (I hope) too much disruption.

Micha, Emunah, Ariella, and Sarah Danziger, shared Mommy with the computer and stayed on my team through the whole process. Also, though they do not realize it, they have helped me immeasurably to clarify my thoughts by asking insightful questions that require straight answers.

I am also grateful to my mother, Mrs. Grace Collins, whose love and support have made my entire life possible.

Betsy Amster, my literary agent, saw the promise in this manuscript and helped to coax that possibility into reality.

I owe a special debt of gratitude to all the clients and students who have submitted writing samples to me over the years and endured the question "What do you *mean*?" scribbled in countless margins.

Alan Snyder, CEO of Answer Financial, Incorporated, urged me to turn the Writamins™ writing tips into a book. Alan's encouragement spurred me to turn a vague idea of "someday" writing a book into the specific reality that the book is today.

Many other friends and colleagues have contributed to this project in a variety of ways deserving of appreciation— some by sharing their insights, some by asking hard questions, and some by helping me find "the point" of living. In particular, my gratitude goes to: Rabbi David Baron, Mrs. Laurie Blumenstrauch, Dr. Devers Branden, Dr. Nathaniel Branden, Mr. Tom Drucker, Mr. William Flicker, Marilyn Hershenson, MSW, Rabbi Daniel Lapin, Rabbi Avi Pogrow, Mr. Jonathan Sadinoff, Dr. Lee Sadja, Dr. Susan Schmidt-Lackner, Marcia Seligson-Drucker, and Mrs. Shelley Zuckerman.

To Becky Cabaza and Sarah Silbert of Three Rivers Press, thank you for your professionalism, intelligence, and good sense. It is a pleasure to work with you.

Finally, to the high school English teacher who once told me, "You will *never* become a writer!", I can say that I let your opinion stop me for a while, but not forever.

CONTENTS

Get to the Point!

WHY DO WE WRITE?

Whether you write business letters, proposals, reports, or any other business messages, you will be glad you read this book. Even better, everyone who reads what you write will be glad you read it, because business readers today have neither the time nor the patience to decode a message that doesn't get right to the point. Getting to the point means getting your point—your idea, proposal, or request—into the mind of your reader.

You may not realize it, but you practice mental telepathy every day. When you write, you transmit your thoughts to others, using nothing but a bunch of little symbols on paper or a computer screen. Only human beings can convey meaning through words. Even the smartest dolphin or gorilla could not come close to doing what you could do in the second grade. The purpose of this book is to help you use words to carry your ideas into your reader's mind as clearly and quickly as possible. *Get to the Point* will help you clarify your meaning and choose the words that will reach into the minds of your readers.

HOW TO USE THIS BOOK

You can read each of these business writing tips on its own, leaf through the book at random, or look up a point that particularly interests you. You can also read the book straight through from beginning to end. However you decide to use it, this book will guide you through the real process of writing—from the moment when you feel the urge to run screaming from the task, through the process of envisioning and then crafting your message, to helping you correct grammar, punctuation, style, and flow.

The book begins with a section on managing your mind. If your mind freezes at the prospect of writing, you're going to have a hard time getting to the point. After offering you practical tools for overcoming writer's block and procrastination, Part Two gives you specific, flexible tools you can use to establish a plan for communicating your message successfully. You will see that identifying your purpose, your reader, and your main point before you begin to write will give you the jump-start you need. Part Three provides powerful techniques to help you structure your information effectively. Part Four covers format—the essential information you need in order to dress your documents for success. Part Five offers you ten ways to build strong sentences. Part Six helps you choose the right words to use—and spot the words to delete.

Parts Seven and Eight cover the subject that most writing books put first: grammar and punctuation. Rules of grammar, spelling, and punctuation are certainly important. However, the success of your writing depends far more on your ability to focus your thoughts, overcome your fears, and pour out sentences that will carry your meaning to your reader. If you become too focused on the rules, you might lose track of the feelings and ideas that you originally intended to convey. I've put the section on grammar and punctuation *after* the sections on planning, organizing, and generating a first draft so that you can write first and worry later.

Part Nine helps you develop the ability to "re-vise"— literally, to see your work again and to adapt it to the perspective of your reader. Part Ten is a sampling of words and phrases that are commonly misused, along with several principles that you can apply to prevent yourself from making these embarrassing mistakes.

Part 1.
MASTERING YOUR MENTAL BARRIERS ABOUT WRITING

Your mind is your most powerful word processor. If it is not working clearly and efficiently, having a super-charged computer will not increase your work output at all. Your great technology will just enable you to produce bad writing more quickly—and in more fonts—than you could before. Effective writing depends on mindset, attitude, emotional state, expectations, and ability to cope with self-criticism. That is why we will begin with the issues that are usually the first ones to confront the writer: fear, loathing, and the overwhelming urge to do anything other than write.

The second part of this section addresses some broader issues that cause writers to stumble. These points appear here because they are part of the mindset that enables you to write more clearly.

OVERCOMING YOUR FEAR OF WRITING

Courage is resistance to fear, mastery of fear—not absence of fear.
> —Mark Twain

If fear, unconsciousness, and a compulsive urge to return phone calls, water plants, or eat cookies are preventing you from sitting down to write, you are not alone. In fact, the only people who never feel apprehensive about writing seem to be the ones who've had frontal lobotomies. These suggestions will help you relieve your fear of writing—without having brain surgery.

1. Take a few deep breaths.

Fear and anxiety cause the abdominal muscles to tense up, forcing the breath to become fast and shallow. This is a throwback to the happy days when our ancestors fled from saber-tooth tigers instead of writing deadlines. Neither fight nor flight are viable options anymore. We must bypass our primitive instincts and get some oxygen into our brains where it might help us think of something to write. Take a few really deep breaths. Slowly. Exhale completely and then inhale completely. You will feel calmer—I promise.

2. Weigh the costs and benefits.

Ask yourself, "What is the worst thing that could happen to me as a result of writing this?" Sure, you could write the letter and then get fired or die, but how likely is that? As much as you may dread writing, odds are that the consequences of *not* writing will be far worse than the consequences of writing. That's a cheery thought, isn't it?

3. Reward yourself after you've reached a certain point in the work.

Take a break or call someone you love or read the next chapter of a trashy novel. (Just make sure that your "break" doesn't eat up the rest of the time you'd set aside for writing.) Don't wait until every last detail is done before you take a brief time-out. Interim incentives and interim rewards will help you nurse yourself through the project. You can still celebrate when the job is complete.

4. Try to allow yourself enough time.

Time pressure only adds to your anxiety. Whenever possible, create a schedule that will have you *finishing* your project several days before the deadline. Then if you hit an unavoidable delay, you won't lose your mind.

5. Schedule time for writing every day.

Professional writers know that if they wait for the writing urge to strike, they might spend the rest of their lives at Starbucks. You cannot wait until you "have time" to sit down and write. You and I both know that there are always other things you could do. If you must finish a writing task, then reserve an hour or so in each day's schedule during which time you will do nothing but write. Try to schedule your writing time at the time of day when you are most alert.

6. Just do it!

"The artist is nothing without the gift, but the gift is nothing without the work," wrote Emile Zola. Sit down and write during the time you've scheduled, whether you want to or not. Don't stop to edit, berate yourself, or harbor homicidal fantasies about the person who assigned you this job until you have completed the task you assigned yourself for the day.

AND YOU THOUGHT YOU HAD PROBLEMS!

Anything that isn't writing is easy.
                —Jimmy Breslin

Many people think that they are the only ones who are nervous about writing, or that professional writers who are "good with language" have an easier time of it. Not true. John Steinbeck, author of *The Grapes of Wrath*, which is widely regarded as the great American novel, suffered from agonies of self-doubt.

John Steinbeck's notebooks from the time he was writing *The Grapes of Wrath* were published in 1989 under the title *Working Days: The Journals of the Grapes of Wrath*. The following excerpts were quoted in *The New York Times Book Review* in April 1989.

> No one else knows my lack of ability the way I do . . .
> Sometimes, I seem to do a good little piece of work,
> but when it is done it slides into mediocrity . . . Got her
> done. And I'm afraid she's a little dull . . . my many

weaknesses are beginning to show their heads . . . my work is no good, I think—I'm desperately upset about it . . . I'm slipping. I've been slipping all my life . . . young man wants to talk, wants to be a writer. What could I tell him? Not a writer myself yet. . . . I am sure of one thing—it isn't the great book I had hoped it would be. It's just a run-of-the-mill book. And the awful thing is that it is absolutely the best I can do.

Reviewer Wilham Kennedy notes:

He wrote the book in five months . . . writing in long-hand and producing 2,000 words a day, the equivalent of seven double-spaced typed pages, an enormous output for any writer, and ultimately a daily tour de force. But he was flagellating himself for this also: 'vacillating and miserable . . . I'm so lazy, so damned lazy. Where has my discipline gone? Have I lost control? My laziness is overwhelming.' This novel would be his ninth work of fiction in 10 years, and he would be 37 years old at its publication.

The main difference between people who write successfully and those who write unsuccessfully is how they respond to their anxiety and resistance. Steinbeck felt it and wrote the *Grapes of Wrath* anyway. The rest of us feel it, and we can hardly concentrate long enough to write *Dear Sir*. The good news is that we don't have to write the great American novel. Finishing today's proposal or report is enough.

AND YOU NEED A HAIRCUT, TOO! STILLING THE INNER CRITIC

I've suffered a great many catastrophes in my life. Most of them never happened.
                                                —Mark Twain

I had writer's block for two years before I wrote my first book. Within a few months of finishing college, I knew that I was going to write a book. Every time I sat down to work, I arranged all my papers, with outline on desk and pen in hand. Words came to mind and I stretched my hand toward the paper. The words seemed to flow from my brain to my forearm, and then they began to slow down. "That is so stupid!" sneered a little voice in my head. I tried to push the words through my wrist into my hand. "That is verbose! How could you even think of writing that?" screeched the critical voice. For two years, I listened to that voice and said, "Gee, you're right. It is stupid. What was I thinking? I can't write that."

One day I sat down to write and my inner critic started its usual number. But this time I mentally turned to that little sucker and said, "Okay! Maybe it is terrible. If it is, I'll throw it away before I show it to anyone. But could we please write *something?*" Stunned into silence, the inner critic retreated. My first book, *The Hand Book,* was published less than two years later. It has since been published in four languages.

Everyone has some kind of internal critic. If you want to write smoothly, you will have to come to terms with yours. Trying to silence the inner critic is fruitless; the more you try to shut it up, the louder it will yell. When it starts to nag you, just say, "Uh huh. Uh huh. Thank you for sharing that. I'll keep that in mind when I revise." And keep working.

GET OFF THE (WRITER'S) BLOCK

Writing is easy. All you do is stare at a sheet of blank paper until drops of blood begin to form on your forehead.
    —Gene Fowler

If you find yourself sitting in front of your computer in a cold sweat, wondering if this is what it feels like to be catatonic, these techniques might help.

1. Use free writing.

Begin by writing whatever comes into your mind. You might begin by typing something like "I can't think of anything to write. My boss is going to kill me if I don't finish this today, and my head feels like a block of granite. . . ." After a few lines of fussing, your brain will probably kick into gear and you'll start writing what you're supposed to write. If several days go by and you are still pouring out your emotional distress, you should probably seek professional assistance. And I don't mean hiring a secretary.

2. Retype the previous day's pages.

If you are writing a new section of a long document, go back to the pages you wrote most recently. Begin retyping those pages. This will give you a running start on the next section.

3. Promise yourself anonymity.

"The only competition worthy of a wise man is with himself," wrote Washington Allston. Remember that no one else will read this but you. Promise yourself that if what you write is awful, you'll delete it or throw it away, and no one will ever have to know it existed.

HITTING THE WALL

Who can make the muddy water clear? Let it be still, and it will gradually become clear.
         —Lao-tzu, *Tao Te Ching*

Let's face it: Sometimes you do run into the mental equivalent of a blank wall. Either you can't remember why you were writing, or you remember but you just don't care anymore. This experience seems to be more common among fiction writers (or maybe they just complain about it more). But it plagues even those of us who have to write progress reports, letters, and proposals. We just get a lot less sympathy.

If you've really hit bottom, there's no point in sitting at your desk trying to force yourself to think. Writing is an intellectual, perhaps even a spiritual exercise. Once you have reached a certain point of mental exhaustion, your mind stops working. The more you try to force yourself to think about your topic, the more stubbornly it keeps replaying the closing scene of *The Godfather* or the final play in last Sunday's football game.

Obviously, you can't lie around waiting for the Muse of the Memo to tell you what to write. You do have to try to jump-start your creativity. However, if you've already pushed all your mental buttons (including the panic button) and you are still staring disconsolately at your computer, just admit that for the moment, the writing part of your brain has vanished into an alternate universe. For those moments when your eyes glaze over completely, here are a few suggestions:

1. **If you are tired, rest.**

Sleep deprivation dulls the brightest wit. Take a short nap and then look at your project again.

2. **Get some exercise.**

A brisk walk, run, or swim will clear your mind and spirit.

3. **Reread your information sources.**

A new idea might strike you.

4. **Remind yourself of your purpose, your key reader, and your core idea.**

You may feel re-inspired.

5. **Discuss the project with someone you trust.**

Speaking with a friend will bring you back into the flow of your subject. It will also relieve the loneliness that comes from working alone fruitlessly.

WHY DO TODAY WHAT YOU NEED TO DO TODAY?

The hardest thing about writing is that first you have to clean the refrigerator.
        —Ernest Hemingway

The urge to procrastinate strikes everyone: The trick is not to let that urge control your actions. Procrastination takes many forms; of course, the best ones are those that actually look like work. Who could fault you for returning phone calls, deleting saved messages from e-mail, and sorting papers? As you busily punch buttons on your telephone, only you will know that you actually have a proposal, report, or letter due by the end of the day and you haven't started it yet.

In addition to doing pseudo-work, you might choose one of the personal-maintenance methods of postponing your encounter with the naked page: getting a drink of water, using the bathroom again, smoking a cigarette, buying a snack, or getting another cup of coffee. The coffee gambit is especially useful if it requires you to leave your office and go to the coffee bar that makes the special latté that helps you think more clearly. When you've exhausted all these methods, you can resort to pointless activities like watering the plants on your desk (even if they're artificial), reading the newspaper, or interrupting someone who is actually trying to work.

Why am I so familiar with all these forms of avoiding writing? Because I've done them all! Here are a few techniques that helped me shake the mañana syndrome. They might help you.

1. Make an appointment with your reader.

If a client were waiting for you in the lobby, would you keep him or her waiting while you returned phone calls and rearranged papers on your desk? Probably not. Think of your writing time as time that you have committed to spend with your reader. Block out writing time in your schedule and then honor that commitment as if your reader had arrived in person to get your message. You'll stay on task more effectively.

2. Break the task into manageable chunks.

How do you eat an elephant? One bite at a time. Writing a 100-page report may seem overwhelming, but drafting an outline or filling in a small section of the outline seems manageable. Create many interim goals and hack away at them one by one.

3. "Just Say No" to your inner child.

Sure, you need to be able to listen to your inner child—but sometimes you have to tell it to shut up. If your procrastination is getting out of control, your inner parent may need to have a little talk with your inner child. The inner child is the voice in your head who seems to be jumping around saying, "I can't write until I have more cookies!" The inner adult is the one who says, "Forget it! You can stop working when you finish this section of the report!"

There's no shame in wanting to stave off a writing project. The greatest writers have shared that desire. Just don't delay too long: Time flies, even if you're not having fun.

COMPLEX IDEAS DEMAND SIMPLE EXPRESSION

You see, wire telegraph is a kind of a very, very long cat. You pull his tail in New York and his head is meowing in Los Angeles. Do you understand this? And radio operates exactly the same way: you send signals here, they receive them there. The only difference is that there is no cat.

—Albert Einstein

Writers often maintain that difficult subjects require difficult language. *I can't possibly explain this simply—it's too complicated.* This rationalization seems to justify writing dense, jargon-laden documents that can only be understood by readers who are already experts on your subject. Unfortunately, the responsibility for successful communication rests with the sender of the message more than on the receiver. In short, if your reader can't understand your complicated idea, it's *your* fault for not explaining it clearly enough.

The Nobel Prize–winning physicist Richard Feynman was once asked to review an introductory physics book. Feynman commented to the author that the book had not fully explained a particular physics concept. "That is too hard for freshman students to understand," said the author. Feynman replied, "If you can't explain it so that a freshman could understand it, then *you* don't understand it." In fact, even the most difficult subjects can be expressed in clear and simple language. And the more difficult your subject matter, the more simple and straightforward your language should be. By using simpler language for complex subject matter, you minimize the net difficulty for your reader. Here are three simple ways to make complex material easier for your reader to understand.

1. Do not use technical terms or jargon.

The jargon is probably the reason that the reader couldn't understand you in the first place.

2. Write sentences that are fewer than 15 words long.

If you have a tough concept to explain, feed it to your reader in small bites.

3. Don't explain one complex idea in terms of another one.

For example, take a sentence like "Stellar nucleosynthesis of trans-boron elements proceeds under pressure only because of a short-lived resonance of beryllium 8." How helpful is this going to be to someone who doesn't understand "short-lived resonance of beryllium 8"?

Begin by referring to something that your reader *does* understand. (Note the quotation from Albert Einstein at the beginning of this section.) Then carry your reader with you from this known territory into the unknown.

When you think that you just *can't* explain that abstract idea simply, remember this adage:

Knowledge is the process of piling up facts; wisdom lies in their simplification.

PUT THE CAUSE BEFORE THE EFFECT

It all started when she hit me back.
>—Anonymous five-year-old child

Business writers often obfuscate their ideas unnecessarily by reversing the natural flow of cause and effect. The notion that cause precedes effect is one of the most powerful patterns of our mental conditioning. When presented with a statement that puts the effect before the cause, the reader's first impulse is to put the information back into cause–effect order. When you bury the cause at the *end* of a statement, you force the reader to reverse the order of the information mentally before he or she can fully comprehend it. The reader will mentally reorganize the concept so that the cause comes before the effect. This process takes effort and time. It often forces readers to reread your work. Why make their lives more difficult?

State the cause of the situation you are describing before you state the effect. For example, compare

> The firm's failure to deliver the product on time, combined with the fact that the product was the wrong color and did not work, led to the loss of this important customer.

to

> The firm lost this important customer because its products did not work as promised, and because they delivered their products late, in the wrong color.

Stating causes clearly requires writers to acknowledge their own actions or errors and to place responsibility squarely on others when necessary. Maybe this is why so many people are loath to put causes first.

If you develop the habit of putting effects before causes, you might unwittingly omit the cause when you are in a hurry or are trying to streamline your work. However, your readers need to understand causes, because comprehending the causes of problems helps them find more intelligent solutions. When you remove the cause, you leave your reader with a fact—an effect—without any explanation of what led to that effect. If you want your reports and analyses to be useful to your readers, *emphasize causes*.

Some sentence constructions lend themselves naturally to burying causes. Try to avoid them.

PROBLEM: Putting the effect before the cause.	SOLUTION: Rework the sentence so that the cause precedes the effect.
"B is due to A."	"A led to B."
"B is caused by A."	"A caused B."
"B was the result of A."	"A caused B," or "A led to B."
"B can be attributed to A."	"A led to B."

Part 2.

PLANNING YOUR WRITING

"Begin with the end in mind" is based on the principle that all things are created twice. There's a mental or first creation, and a physical or second creation to all things.
　　　　　　　—Stephen Covey

PLAN YOUR WORK—THEN WORK YOUR PLAN

Have you ever set off late for a meeting in a place you've never visited before, without looking at a map before you left? As you head down the street, the thought crosses your mind: "Maybe I should look at a map." And then you say to yourself, "I don't have *time* to look at a map! I have to keep moving!" Then you end up careening past your highway turnoff at 75 miles per hour as you struggle to read a map that is perched on the steering wheel. Most people have a similar approach to the process of writing. They know they ought to plan their document or draft an outline, but they don't have *time*. They plunge directly into a tête-à-tête with the computer screen or paper, little knowing that by *not* planning their work, they may be doubling the total time their project will require.

The battle for clarity is won or lost during the planning stage, long before you write your first draft. Effective planning enables you to clarify *why* you are writing, *what* you want to say, and *how* you intend to make your message understandable for your reader. During my 20 years as a writer, editor, and writing trainer, I have seen that ineffective (or nonexistent) planning capsizes more writing projects than any other factor—more than ignorance about grammar, more than stilted writing style, more than an inability to revise.

When you plan your document, you set the trajectory for your message, aiming it toward your specific reader. Send it off course at this stage and your message will not connect—even if every word is perfectly spelled. When you finish planning and organizing, the essence of the project is established—for better or for worse.

Anything worth writing is worth planning. In fact, anything worth doing is worth planning, but I don't want to start sounding like your mother. The good news is that organizing your ideas does not take much time. Spend a few minutes planning before you write, and you will save yourself hours of painful revision at the end.

HOW TO BUDGET YOUR WRITING TIME

If I had eight hours to chop down a tree, I'd spend six sharpening my axe.

—Abraham Lincoln

The answer to the question "What part of the writing process takes the most time?" seems to be a no-brainer. Obviously, writing takes the most time (unless you count procrastinating, which can take years). The fact is, however, that the majority of the time spent on any writing project should be spent preparing to write. Assume that you will spend about 40 percent of your total writing time clarifying your purpose, analyzing your reader, gathering your information, and brainstorming your points. Breezing through your first draft should take about 15 percent of your time.

Once you have something on paper, you'll spend the remainder of your time going through the stages of revision that you'll discover in Part 9, "Re-Vision Means Seeing Again."

GETTING READY TO WRITE: THE THREE P'S

For every minute spent in organizing, an hour is earned.
        —Source Unknown

Whether you are writing or speaking, knowing what *you* mean to say is not enough; you have to get that meaning into another person's head, preferably without using any sharp utensils. If you send a memo asking 40 sales representatives to submit their call logs by Friday morning, and on Friday afternoon you've received call logs from five people and expense reports from seven others, then, in effect, you did not ask them to submit those call logs by Friday. Your communication did not work because somehow, your request did not register with the people who were expected to understand it.

It would be fun to put all the blame on those darned readers when a message fails to connect, but a big chunk of responsibility falls on the writer too. If your readers don't respond, you must assume that your message was not mean-ingful *to them*. Many people forget this when they write. They throw a lot of information onto the paper and let the reader keep whatever he can catch. This is not the kind of writing that inspires or interests the person who is spending precious time to read what you wrote.

In the next few pages, you'll learn about a process called *the three P's*. The three P's are *purpose, person*, and *point*. The three P's correspond to the three elements of every communi-cation: sender, receiver, and message. Clarifying your purpose helps you refine your intentions as the sender. Analyzing your reader raises the likelihood that the reader—your receiver—will understand you. Honing your point helps you refine your message. If you clarify the three P's, you can be confident that your document will contain the essentials of successful communication.

KNOW YOUR PURPOSE BEFORE YOU START

Firmness of purpose is one of the most necessary sinews of character, and one of the best instruments of success. Without it genius wastes its efforts in a maze of inconsistencies.
—Lord Chesterfield

The clearer you are about your purpose, the more likely you are to fulfill it. Everything about your document flows from its purpose: word choice, organization, and format. When try-ing to clarify your purpose, ask yourself:

- Why am I writing this?
- What result do I intend it to produce?

- How do I want my reader to think, feel, or act as a result of reading it?

Some common purposes of documents include:

Inform	Persuade	Request	Warn
Promise	Confirm	Deny	Recommend

Most documents contain information, but that does not mean their primary purpose is to inform. If you want your reader to think or feel differently, then your purpose is probably to persuade. If you want your reader to take some action, then your purpose is probably to request.

REQUESTS PRODUCE ACTION

Imagine this scene: A married woman comes home from work, kicks off her shoes, flings herself on the couch, and groans, "I had an awful day today." How is her husband likely to respond? "Sorry to hear that, honey. Let's go to a nice restaurant for dinner." or "Oh. What's for dinner?" I have posed this question to audiences all over the United States. Most of the hapless men choose option two ("What's for dinner?"), only to be met with derision from every woman in the room. Why does this happen so predictably? Because the men assume that when the woman says, "I had an awful day," she is simply sharing a piece of information. Although this is technically true, most of the women realize that "I had an awful day" is actually a coded message. It means, "If you loved me, you'd take me out to dinner." This message seems so obvious that most wives assume it doesn't need to be spoken. This assumption causes domestic strife throughout the world.

Making unspoken or indirect requests causes many problems in private life, but it also leads to lost profits and increased confusion in business. For example, one of my clients hired a shipping company to transport its products overseas. Some of the products had been damaged in transit. A participant in my writing seminar had been told to report the loss to the shipping company and request reimbursement for the lost cargo. She turned in her letter as a writing sample. It went something like this:

> Dear Sirs:
>
> On November 9, 199_, your company shipped [cargo] from our manufacturing plant to [destination]. When the cargo arrived, several boxes of [product] had been torn open; the merchandise in these boxes had been damaged so that it could not be sold. The value of the lost merchandise was $532.55. I look forward to hearing from you at your earliest convenience so that we may resolve this matter.
>
> Yours truly,

When I asked the person who wrote this letter what its purpose was, she replied, "To get the money back." Reread the letter and ask yourself what's missing. You'll notice that the letter does not contain a request for reimbursement. In fact, it contains no request at all. It informs the reader of the lost merchandise, of the value of that merchandise, and of the fact that the writer looks forward to receiving a call. A brief request would have clarified the company's position. "Please reimburse us $532.55 to replace the merchandise that your company damaged in transit." Without this simple statement, the shipping company has not even been asked to refund the money.

If your purpose is to produce action, then your purpose is to *request*. If you want your reader to do something by a particular time, you must ask for exactly what you want and clearly state the time and date by which you need to receive it. Naturally, your writing cannot be a long list of "gimmes." You may need to add supporting information to explain why your request is reasonable.

Here are a few key points about requests.

- Every request must include a definite deadline, which is the time by which you expect the request to be fulfilled. Asking someone to respond "as soon as possible" is asking for trouble. If the reader wants to, he can decide that the "soonest possible" time to respond would be some time next year. If what you mean is *please return it by Friday at 5:00 P.M.*, then you do not mean *as soon as possible*. You mean *Friday at 5:00 P.M.* Say so.
- Verbalize your request as specifically as you can. For example, write *please send us the application forms* rather than *we need to receive the application forms*. Note that the second sentence is not a request at all; it's a statement of information about what *we* need. Please *send, call, write, visit, attend*—whatever action you expect, specify it in your document.
- If you make the request at the beginning or in the middle of a letter, restate it at the end. This will remind the

reader (who has already forgotten the beginning of the letter) that there was something he was supposed to do.

PERSON: ANALYZE YOUR READER BEFORE YOU START

You can make more friends in two months by becoming interested in other people than you can in two years by trying to get other people interested in you.
          —Dale Carnegie

Writers sometimes forget about their readers when they sit down to write. They put so much tension and effort into getting words onto paper that they lose sight of the fact that writing is much more than creating orderly lines of letters and symbols. Writing is a way of developing a relationship with another person: your reader. The only way that you can achieve your **purpose** is to transmit your **point** to the **person** who will receive your message. If your reader does not grasp the meaning of your words, then, in effect, you did not write.

Regardless of how you feel about your reader, whether you like him or loathe him, respect him or despise him, you are utterly dependent on him for the ultimate success of your communication. Your message goes nowhere and does nothing unless your reader understands it. Only when your reader decodes your message and re-creates your meaning within his or her mind have you completed your communication. In short, the reader gets the final vote about whether you communicated and about the message you have conveyed.

CONNECTING, CONNECTING, CONNECTING

How can you maximize the likelihood that your reader will grasp your meaning? By connecting with him at several levels simultaneously.

LEVEL ONE: FUNDAMENTAL

- Use a language that he understands. (If you tell a group of Americans an obscene joke in Swahili, is the joke obscene?) Choose words that the reader understands. Avoid technical jargon.
- Structure your sentences at a level that is appropriate to the reader's educational background.

LEVEL TWO: JUST MENTAL

Answer the questions that the reader is likely to be asking himself about **your message.**

- Why does this matter *to me?*
- What could I *gain* by responding to this information?
- What could I *lose* by ignoring it?
- What am I supposed to *do* about it?

LEVEL THREE: HEAVY MENTAL

Answer the questions that the reader is probably asking himself about **you:**

- Are you trustworthy?
- Are you competent?
- What authority do you have?

Harness the reader's attention at all these levels—from the simple level of understanding your words to the deeper level of believing you to be sincere and of giving weight to your statements. You will maximize your chances of communicating successfully.

Your analysis of your reader will affect the vocabulary, tone, and even the content of your message. When you have a variety of points or pieces of information to choose from, decide which points will be most significant and persuasive to your reader. You probably will not change your main point; however, you may choose to vary the emphasis and phrasing depending on the passions of your reader.

Before you begin, take a few moments to think carefully about the human being to whom you are writing. Considering that your message rises or falls based on that person's willingness and capacity to understand you, the time you spend pondering your reader will be well spent.

TARGET YOUR READER'S HOT BUTTONS

All people have "hot buttons"—topics that charge them with emotional energy and motivate them to act. People may act to gain a pleasure associated with a particular subject or to avoid a pain associated with a negative one. "Touching a hot button" means alluding or referring to a topic that has emotional power for your reader.

Before you start to write, consider what you know about your reader. What does he care passionately about? What is his greatest fear? What is his greatest hope? Think about the forces that drive your reader; this will help you target areas of emotional impact. Your assessment of the reader's nature will affect your decision about which points to include and how to organize those points in your document.

Most people are motivated either by *fear* and the attempt to avoid pain or by *love* and the attempt to gain pleasure. Before you decide which hot buttons to emphasize for your reader, ask yourself whether this is a person who is more motivated by avoiding pain or by getting pleasure. Is he willing to risk his current security in order to pursue a potential gain, or does he cling to what he has for fear of losing it?

Here are a few common hot buttons:

NEGATIVE HOT BUTTONS

- Loss of money
- Criticism
- Recurring problems
- Loss of reputation
- Public embarrassment
- Bankruptcy
- High debt levels
- Unnecessary costs
- Lawsuits

POSITIVE HOT BUTTONS

- Profit
- Praise
- Saving time
- Gaining market share

- Enhancing reputation
- Productivity
- Power or control
- Gaining reliability
- Gaining accuracy

If several people will read your document, target the hot buttons of the key decision-maker. If your document must pass through a gatekeeper such as a secretary or administrative assistant before it reaches your key decision-maker, then insert a cover letter in which you briefly outline the value of the document to the decision maker.

> You may have many potential points. Choose those that are most likely to help you fulfill your purpose and meet your reader's needs.

SO WHAT'S THE POINT?

If you can't write your idea on the back of a business card, you don't know what your idea is.
              —Maxwell Perkins

No matter how many facts or details your document may contain, there is **one** fundamental message that you are trying to convey. This main point is the one you must clarify for yourself before you start to write. Even a document that is hundreds of pages long can generally be abstracted into one key point if the document is cogently written. For example, the key point of this book is that you must always write with your reader in mind.

Before you begin to write, ask yourself, "What is my basic point?" Think carefully: What is the *one point* without which you will be unable to fulfill your purpose? What one point most embodies your message in a way that will touch your reader? If you are finding it difficult to clarify your main point, ask yourself:

- What am I really trying to say?
- If I had to boil this down to one sentence, what would that sentence be?
- If I only had 30 seconds to deliver my message, what would I say?

You might not express your main point in your document in the same way that you phrase it to yourself. However, it is essential that you know what the fundamental point is.

Too often, writers begin with a plethora of points. Unsure about which one is most central, they throw all of them onto the paper and pray that the reader will figure out which one is most important. I have news for those of you who use this method: If you don't know which one is the main point, your reader won't either. And if your reader doesn't understand you, then what's the point?

CONNECT PURPOSE, PERSON, AND POINT

In theory, there is no difference between theory and practice. But in practice, there is.
        —Jan L.A. van de Snepscheut

The points you choose are a natural outgrowth of your assessment of your purpose and your reader. To illustrate how assessing the reader affects the way you choose your points, let's imagine that you are writing a proposal to the owner of a small Caribbean island that you want to buy. Thus, your *purpose* is to persuade the owner to sell the island to you.

Now let's imagine two very different individuals who might be reading this proposal. First, imagine that the owner of the island is a little old lady who lives on a neighboring island that her family has owned for generations and who is dedicated to protecting the environment. She's 90 years old. Some of her grandchildren have moved away to the city; some of them still enjoy swimming and fishing on their private family island. She has always intended to leave the island to her grandchildren. She must answer to her descendants and satisfy her sense of loyalty to her ancestors. What are some of this reader's hot buttons? What factors will influence her? The answers to these questions will help you decide what points to include.

OWNER'S HOT BUTTONS: 90-YEAR-OLD MATRIARCH

1. Financial security for her extended family.

2. Conservation of the island's beauty.

3. Respect for the island, its history, and her ancestors.

Now imagine a different owner. Suppose that a large conglomerate owns the island. It uses the facilities there for off-site meetings and for employees' bonus vacations. In this scenario, your reader is the CFO of a major corporation—a person with financial savvy and training who knows he must justify his opinions to upper management and to stockholders. Maybe profits have been down recently, or his employees have started grumbling, "Oh no, not the Caribbean again!" when they get word of their bonus vacations. Maybe the company is doing extremely well and needs to take a loss for tax purposes. What are some of *this* reader's hot buttons? What would motivate him?

OWNER'S HOT BUTTONS: CORPORATE CFO

1. Tax advantages to selling the property.
2. Desire to continually upgrade the company's incentive compensation plan for high-performing employees.
3. Opportunity to eliminate a significant cost center.

The *purpose* of the proposal to either reader is the same: to persuade the owner to sell the island. However, you can see that the *points* you raise in your proposal will vary dramatically depending on your reader.

That's the power of using the three P's—when you know and understand these three components of your communication, you can target your reader much more precisely than would otherwise be possible.

USING THE THREE P'S

Think about a document that you need to write soon.
Answer these questions about it:

Project: _____

1. What is my *purpose* in writing this? What result or action do I intend it to produce?

2. What *person* is going to read this? Will he or she understand all the technical terms? What ideas might need explanation? What *hot buttons* should I allude to?

3. If I had to tell the basic *point* of this document in one sentence, what would that sentence be? (Boil it down!)

4. What other points should I include in order to make my work complete?

After you've finished this exercise, you are ready to move on to the next step in the writing process: organizing your information in a way that will help you fulfill your purpose by conveying your point most persuasively to your reader.

From *Get to the Point!* by Elizabeth Danziger, copyright © 2001 by Elizabeth Danziger (Three Rivers Press). This page may be photocopied for individual use only.

Part 3.

ORGANIZING INFORMATION EFFECTIVELY

Organizing is what you do before you do something, so that when you do it, it is not all mixed up.
   —A. A. Milne

If you organize your material well, your reader will sense that you have thought carefully about your subject. Moreover, organizing your information gives you a sense of control over your subject and enables you to be as clear and complete as possible.

FORM FOLLOWS FUNCTION

If you were designing a product such as a chair or a blender, you'd begin with the question "What do I want it to do?" It would be obvious that a chair should be designed so that someone can sit on it and that a blender should be able to blend foods. The next questions would flow naturally from the question of function. "In order for it to do what I want it to do, what form should it take? What parts does it need?" It's unlikely that you would choose the shape for the item first and then consider what the item is supposed to do. If you did, you might end up with chairs that no one could sit on or blenders that look great in the kitchen but can't frappé. Form follows function in written documents too.

In school, you may have been taught to follow a particular form in every letter or report, regardless of the function of the particular document. There seemed to be some inherent virtue in writing reports that followed the classic I. A 1. a. (1) (a) outline, even though using this structure might mean cutting your ideas to fit the form. At some point in your career, you might have been told to begin every report with a subhead called *Background*, even when your readers already knew the background or couldn't care less about it. No matter how well your outline conforms to a predetermined pattern, it will not carry your idea if it does not suit your message.

ORGANIZING AND WRITING: WHAT'S THE DIFFERENCE?

Readers may not differentiate between writing and organizing errors; they will just know that they develop an overpowering urge to run away when your document is in their hand. However, as a writer, you need to know that organizing and writing are separate processes, each of which has a profoundly different impact on the quality of your final draft. Organizing problems take the form of poor sequencing of ideas, omission of ideas, redundancy, irrelevancy, jerky transitions, and so forth. Writing problems include errors in grammar, spelling, and punctuation. Writing errors and organizing errors have different causes and require different solutions.

The key difference between writing and organizing problems is this: Writing problems are constant throughout a document, while organizing problems get worse as you go along. If you receive a one-page document that has many spelling errors, you can reasonably expect to see the same level of spelling errors in a 20-page document from the same writer. If someone sends you a one-page document that is poorly organized, you will probably be able to make sense of it by reorganizing the information in your head. However, if someone sends you a 20-page document that is not well organized, you will be completely befuddled long before you reach the last page.

> **Organize your ideas in a lucid, clear manner. Fulfill your purpose and meet the needs of your reader. If you do not, your message will be lost, no matter how perfectly you have spelled each word or how carefully you have chosen your font.**

MAIN POINT FIRST: THE CLASSIC PARAGRAPH STRUCTURE

A sentence expresses a complete thought or a complete part of an idea. A paragraph generally covers a whole topic or a whole aspect of a topic. The classic paragraph structure looks like this:

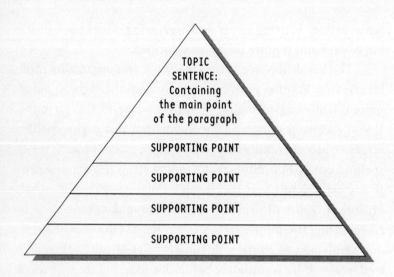

Most readers expect business writing to follow this form. The main point of each paragraph is stated in the topic sentence; and the supporting details justify and elaborate on the main point. Busy readers will find it easier to scan your documents if you provide clear topic sentences for every paragraph. Executives and managers often lack the time to read every document closely. They skim before they decide whether to read the whole document . Sometimes they only read the Executive Summary and the Conclusion. Sometimes they jump from paragraph to paragraph, sucking up each topic sentence and creating a mental image of the whole document. Be sure that your document has clearly delineated paragraphs with rational topic sentences so that your boss or client will be able to track your line of thinking as she jumps from paragraph to paragraph.

PATTERNS OF ORGANIZATION

Man is the great pattern maker and pattern perceiver. No matter how primitive his situation, no matter how tormented, he cannot live in a world of chaos.
        —Edmund Carpenter

There are many logical ways to organize your points. Choose one based on your purpose, on the types and number of points you need to make, and on the needs or requirements of your reader. Here are a few of the ways that you can organize your information.

1. Put your main point first.

People are paying closest attention at the beginning of your document. Give your reader the bottom line first; follow up with reasoning and background. This is the classic "first things first" approach. Use it as your default pattern, deviating from it only when you have a particular reason to use another structure.

> We are strongly opposed to doing business with XYZ Company. The President is a known felon, the Chief Operating Officer has no experience in running a company, the Controller has a history of embezzlement, and the Human Resources Manager was recently arrested for starting a fistfight in a bar.

2. If you don't put the main point first, put it last.

If your reader is likely to oppose your conclusion, build your case gradually and unveil your conclusion at the end. If you lead with a point that will irritate or upset your reader, you

can be fairly sure that he will not read the document through
to its end.

> As you may know, we have added many new features to our
> offices in the past year. We have bought new computers,
> upgraded our software, and hired several technology
> experts to oversee data-processing functions. We have also
> remodeled our lobby; now you can relax in spacious leather
> chairs and enjoy a cup of fresh-ground coffee as you wait
> for your appointment with one of our highly trained profes-
> sionals. To support this improvement in customer service, it
> is necessary that we increase our hourly rates by 20%,
> effective immediately.

3. Describe the situation in chronological order.

When you need to give a history of a situation or a product,
you may need to tell it in chronological order. You can work
from the beginning to the present or trace a situation from
the present to its origins in the past. Accident reports and
progress reports often require this approach.

> This issue came to our attention in June 1999. At that time,
> we realized that employees resented being charged five
> cents for every photocopy they made. The "nickel per copy"
> policy also created a storage problem, as we did not know
> what to do with all the nickels. In August 1999, we dropped
> the price to a penny a copy. However, employees still seemed
> to feel that this policy was unfair. Finally, in March 2001, we
> decided to drop the photocopy charge altogether. As an
> alternative cost-cutting measure, we removed the coffee-
> maker from the company's kitchen.

4. Compare or contrast by making clear distinctions.

If you want to compare advantages and disadvantages of two options, format the page so that the two choices are visually separate. It is painful to read:

Property A has five bedrooms, while Property B has 4 bedrooms. Property A has 3½ baths, but property B has 4. The air conditioning works well in A, but B has a great sea breeze.

Most of the reader's attention will be spent trying to separate the A's from the B's instead of actually analyzing the differences between the two options.

When comparing two sets of information, try to put each set into a separate sentence or paragraph. If you want your reader to compare apples with oranges, put all the apples together and put all the oranges together. Then draw your conclusion regarding similarity or difference of the two things you are comparing in a concluding sentence. By distinguishing the two sets of information clearly and pointing out the implications of their differences, you help your reader to make an intelligent comparison.

Property A

This home has 5 bedrooms, 3½ baths, a living room with a vaulted ceiling, a formal dining room, and a den with a fireplace. It overlooks the Pacific Ocean in Malibu. With new hardwood floors, it is in perfect move-in condition. The listing price is $800,000.

Property B
This home has 6 bedrooms, 4 baths, a living room with a
sunken alcove and fireplace, and a spacious kitchen with
breakfast nook. All the plumbing has been replaced within
the past two years. Nestled high in the Hollywood Hills, it
commands a view of the entire city. The listing price is
$825,000.

5. State the problem and summarize the proposed solution.

Business decisions revolve around problems and their solutions. Analyzing a situation in problem-solution structure will help build your reputation as a problem-solver. Managers are usually problem-oriented, and they appreciate knowing what the problem is (not the background, not the excuses, not the history) and knowing what solution you propose.

Problem: More than 90% of our customers pay their bills
60 to 90 days late.

Solution: We can address this problem in several ways.
We could offer discounts to customers who pay
on time. We could charge interest on accounts
more than 30 days delinquent. We could also
stop shipping to customers who are more than
120 days delinquent.

6. Present information in the sequence in which it will be used.

This is an excellent way to organize instructions, manuals, and descriptions of processes. "First you do this, and then you do that. . . ." Thus you carry your reader through the correct sequence of actions. Try to keep your sentences short.

First, push the "ON" switch on the computer. You will soon see various messages flashing across the screen. After a couple of minutes, you should see what we call an "A prompt." It looks like this: A>. When you see this, type "wp" and then press "Return." This will load your word-processing software, Word Perfect, into the machine. Soon you will see a blank screen with the message "Doc 1 Page 1" at the bottom right. This means that your software is loaded and you are ready to begin work.

Any of these patterns of organization can be effective, depending on your purpose, your reader, and your main point. The Organic Outlining technique presented in the coming pages will help you structure your document successfully.

SIMPLE SPIN DOCTORING

The point of maximum impact is
AT THE BEGINNING.
The point where most people go to sleep is
in the middle.
The point of maximum retention is
AT THE END.

You can convey a positive or negative opinion—without making an overt statement—just by organizing your ideas strategically. This tactic is especially useful if you are in a profession where "covering the derrière" is *de rigueur*.

Strategic organizing succeeds because of a basic fact of communication: in any message, the point of maximum impact is at the beginning and the point of maximum retention is at the end. People are most affected by the information that is presented to them at the *beginning* of a document and are most likely to remember information that is presented to them at the *end*.

Do you want to create a *negative* impression without coming out and making a negative recommendation? Place negative information at the beginning and end, and bury the benefits in the middle. The negatives will stand out in the reader's memory.

Do you want to give a *positive* impression? Place your most favorable information at the beginning and the end, and bury the negatives in the middle. Your reader will come away with a positive impression of the option you have highlighted at the beginning and the end, and you will have avoided making a definite statement.

For example, suppose that someone has asked your opinion about a particular piece of real estate. Let's say that the raw information includes these facts, some positive and some negative:

- Comparable properties in the neighborhood have appreciated consistently over the past five years.
- When the wind blows from the west, unpleasant fumes from a nearby chemical plant sometimes waft over the property.
- The current owner has not maintained the property well.
- The building needs a new roof.
- A local developer plans to build a new "upscale" shopping mall a few miles away from the property.
- The building was designed by a famous local architect and most of the original fixtures are still in place.

Suppose that you think it is a good idea to buy the property. You would open with a positive point (point of maximum impact). You'd bury the negative points in the middle (point where the reader falls asleep), and put another strong positive point at the end (point of maximum retention). Your paragraph might look like this:

Comparable properties in the neighborhood have appreciated consistently over the past five years. A famous local architect designed the building and most of the original fixtures are still in place. Although the current owner has not maintained the property well, the original structure retains its charm. The building needs a new roof and some other minor repairs. A few tenants have mentioned that unpleasant fumes from a nearby chemical plant sometimes waft over the property. However, this happens only on occasional windy days. A local developer plans to build a new "upscale" shopping mall a few miles away from the property. This increased proximity to shopping facilities should increase the desirability of the neighborhood.

Now suppose that you think it is a bad idea to purchase the property. You might write something like this:

This building has not been well maintained by the current owner. It needs a new roof and other repairs. Tenants have complained that when the wind blows from the west, unpleasant fumes from a nearby chemical plant sometimes waft over the property. A well-known local architect designed the building and the original fixtures have never been replaced. Comparable properties in the neighborhood have appreciated consistently over the past five years,

> although this is no guarantee that the growth will continue.
> A local developer plans to build a new "upscale" shopping
> mall a few miles away from the property. This new mall might
> contribute to increased traffic congestion.

The same facts have been presented in both paragraphs. Neither paragraph makes a specific recommendation, yet the paragraphs carry very different connotations.

Just remember: Your reader will retain the last thing that he reads!

THE TWO RULES OF ORGANIC OUTLINING

Here's a useful and important test: Think of any idea—on any subject. Try to convey it to someone without using a sentence. You'll find that it's impossible. This underlines a key principle that topic outlining ignores: It takes a sentence to express an idea. If you learn only one thing about organizing, this should be it.

—Joe Floren

The great sculptor Michelangelo was visiting a marble quarry when he saw an ungainly hunk of rock being loaded onto a sledge. He ran to the quarry workers and cried, "I must have that piece of marble! How much does it cost?"

A workman replied, "We have many blocks of marble the same size. Why do you need this one in particular?"

"Ah," said Michelangelo, "You look at it and see a hunk of stone. I look at it and see the sculpture within it."

Before you write a document—be it a letter, a report, a proposal, or an article—you may feel that you're facing an undifferentiated lump of information and ideas. The prospect of turning that bulky mass of ideas into a balanced, organized written message may seem overwhelming. The Organic Outlining* technique enables you to find and bring forth the message within that mass of information. Traditional outlining requires you to cut and trim your ideas to conform to the classic "I, II, A.B.C." structure. Organic Outlining enables you to shape your message in a way that emerges naturally from your material and connects your purpose, your reader, and your main point.

Before you begin your Organic Outline, you'll need to have plenty of sticky notes such as Post-It™ notes. You'll also need a large surface such as a desk or a blank wall on which to stick those notes.

Organic Outlining has only two rules. If you follow these two rules rigorously, you will be able to do something you might not have thought possible: write a clear, organized, succinct first draft directly from your outline. That's the good news. The bad news is that if you do not follow these rules exactly, your Organic Outline will not perform its magic.

1. Write each idea as a sentence.

Writing each idea as a sentence forces you to compose your ideas as complete thoughts. It weans you off of "grocery list

---

* This technique is adapted from the Diagnostic Outlining™ presented by Joe Floren in his book *Don't Let Your Brain Outrace Your Hand,* published by Twain Productions in Wheaton, Illinois. "Diagnostic Outlining" is a registered service mark of Twain Productions, Wheaton, IL.

outlines." A grocery list outline contains one- or two-word descriptions that don't help you at all when it's time to write. For example, you might write "Market Trends" or "Background" as ideas. These terms are not thoughts; they are "grocery list" topics like "apples or "peanut butter." Sure, "market trends" reminds you that you wanted to say *something* about market trends, but what about them? Are they going up? Going down? Changing in a way that will affect your business? If you had written "Market trends are favorable," you would have a sentence on which to base a paragraph in your first draft. As Joe Floren points out in *Don't Let Your Brain Outrace Your Hand,*

> Grocery list topic outlines are little help in diagnosing problems with sequence, omission, irrelevancy or redundancy of ideas. That's because grocery lists don't deal with ideas, only things. In this sense, topics like *scope, benefits, purpose,* etc. are things. That's why grocery lists only tell you what a report *is about*. They do not tell you what that report *says*. This is a crucial distinction for, unless the outline tells what the report will actually say, you have no chance of telling whether it will say it well or poorly.

Here is another huge advantage of writing each idea as a sentence: It enables you to shift smoothly from the outline stage to the first draft, **because you have already written sentences for each of your outline points.**

2. Put only one idea on each Post-It note or card.

When you put only one idea on each sticky note, you will separate your ideas from the order in which they originally fell out of your brain. Unfortunately, ideas may pour out based on some random pattern of association known only to your unconscious mind. Nevertheless, once two ideas show up next to each other on paper, they begin to seem like they belong together, and you are unlikely to move them. Separate them and mix them up. Then, when you group them into sentences and paragraphs, you can be confident that you are placing these ideas together because they *belong* together, and not just because you happened to think of them at the same time.

Writing each individual idea onto a different sticky note will also make you examine each idea more carefully. Separating each idea makes it easier to find and eliminate redundant or irrelevant points.

Disciplining yourself to write only one idea per sticky note means that you'll write short, chunky sentences. Instead of writing a serpentine sentence and then trying to hack it apart, you will create many short, single-point sentences and then decide whether to link them together. Don't worry—you'll have the opportunity to turn all those brief, concise thoughts into long, convoluted sentences if you want to. However, once you see how nice they look when they are not snaking from line to line, you might decide to keep them short.

Organic Outlining lets you ponder, clarify, and rearrange your ideas *before* they appear next to each other in a draft of the document. Let's see how it works in practice.

ORGANIC OUTLINING IN ACTION

A craftsman carved an extraordinary likeness of a bear out of a hunk of wood. A tourist saw the carving and asked, "How did you make that wood look so much like a bear?"

"It was easy," replied the craftsman, "I just took the hunk of wood and carved away everything that didn't look like a bear."
        —Source Unknown

STEP ONE: LET IDEAS FLOW FROM YOUR MIND.

1. Write *one* idea on each sticky note.
2. Write each idea as a sentence.
3. Scatter the sticky notes on your white-board, wall, or other uncluttered surface in random order.

As additional points come to mind, jot them on sticky notes and put them on your outlining surface. When you are satisfied that you have written all your major points and most significant pieces of supporting information on sticky notes in sentence form, mix them up. Move them around on the board. Don't worry about separating two sticky notes that seem to be related. The points that belong together logically will end up together in the end.

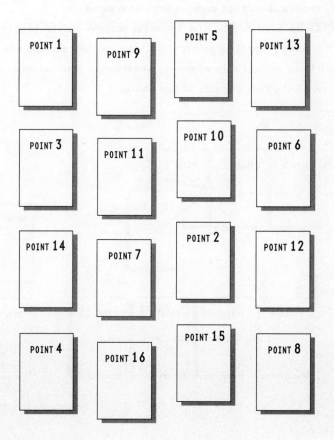

STEP TWO: GROUP MAIN POINTS WITH SUPPORTING POINTS.

1. Identify main points.
2. Place main points on the left side of the board.
3. Choose ideas that support each main point.
4. Group main points and their supporting points together, placing supporting points slightly below their main points.
5. If you are not sure where—or whether—an idea belongs, put it on the far right side of the board.

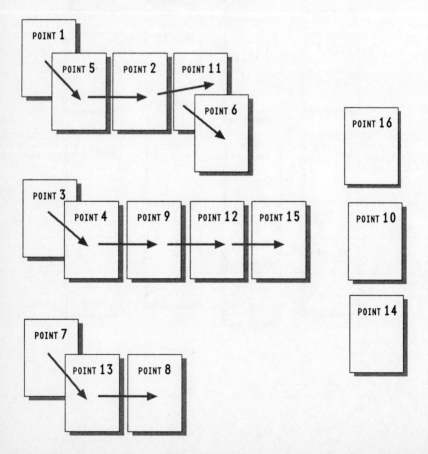

STEP THREE: CHECK FOR OMISSIONS, DUPLICATIONS, OR IRRELEVANT INFORMATION.

OMISSIONS

If one main point has fewer supporting points than the others, you might have omitted an important piece of supporting information. Identify what's missing and create a new supporting point to fill in the gap.

REDUNDANCIES

If one main point has many more points than another, or if the same basic idea appears with slightly different phrasing on several supporting points, you might be repeating yourself. Eliminate the weakest versions.

IRRELEVANT INFORMATION

Look at the "orphan" points on the far right side of the page. Are they really relevant? If you see that they are relevant, group them with their appropriate main point. If not, throw them away. If you can't bear to toss them out, then stick them under your desk or on another wall. Just get them out of your field of vision. Eliminating these unnecessary points now means that you won't have to spot them and weed them out of your first draft.

*   *   *

As you scan your major points, you may find that some have three or more pieces of supporting data, while others have only one or perhaps none. Look hard at the points that lack support. You might need to develop more supporting points for them—or you might decide that they are not actually main points at all.

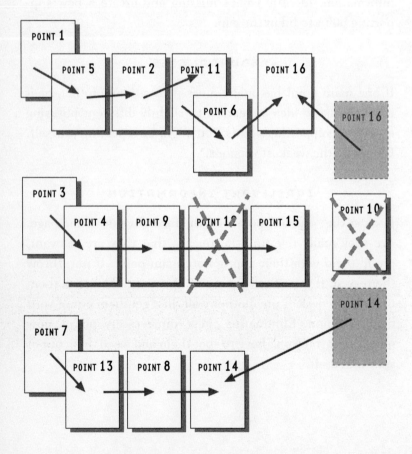

STEP FOUR: EACH MAIN POINT–SUPPORTING POINT GROUP WILL BECOME A PARAGRAPH OF YOUR DOCUMENT.

1. Each main point is the topic sentence of a paragraph.
2. Each supporting point is a sentence of supporting detail.
3. Before you begin your first draft, take a last look at your Organic Outline and ask yourself if the order of the paragraphs suits your purpose. If not, you can lift the entire paragraph grouping and place it in a more appropriate spot.

During this step, you do your first and most important edit of the document. You now have all your major points and sub-points in front of you, laid out so that you can see all of them at a glance. While your document is in this skeletal form, you have the best chance to see its strengths and weaknesses. This is the time to reinforce your strengths and shore up the weaknesses as you develop the structure of the document.

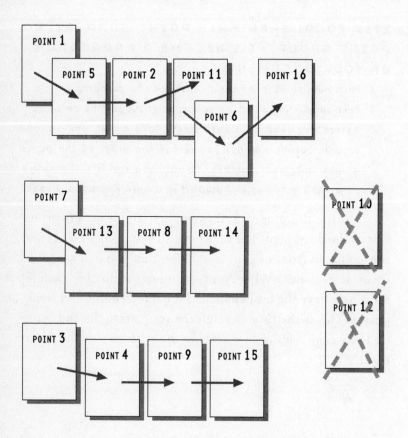

Reconsider your three P's: purpose, person, and point. Are there any blocks of information that will not serve any of the three P's? Even if all the information blocks are relevant, ask yourself *now* what their optimal order is. You can rearrange sets of sticky notes as often as you wish. This process gives you an at-a-glance view of a variety of possible structures. *It is infinitely easier to move around sticky notes than it is to dissect a long document that is already written. Play with the structure until the ideas flow smoothly.*

The beauty of Organic Outlining is that it makes it easy for you to sort, organize, and regroup all of your ideas before you write the first draft.

Why bother? You might think that it would be quicker and easier to plunge straight into composing the first draft without using the sticky notes. All I ask is that you try this technique a few times. You will see for yourself that the time you spend writing ideas on sticky notes is recouped many times over. Being able to look at the whole document at one glance gives you a visual sense of your document's structure in ways that traditional outlining methods cannot offer.

PLANNING A LARGE WRITING PROJECT

If you are writing a letter, memo, or brief report, you can schedule time for it over a few days and follow a basic routine of planning, drafting, revising, and proofreading. However, if you are working on a larger project such as a major presentation, annual report, or proposal for a major contract, you need to schedule more thoroughly. You may be dependent on other people to provide you with essential information. You may need to work with a graphics staff to design visual elements of the document. You may need to schedule photo shoots or interviews with key contributors. All of these steps take time. If you want to use your lead time wisely, plan it carefully.

Many kinds of project-planning software are available to help you plan large-scale productions, but you can probably get by without the software if you remember one key point: *Everything takes longer than it should.* Murphy's Law of Project Planning dictates that countless delivery lags will combine to put you into a state of sleepless, panicked agitation 48 hours before your project is due, *unless you build in time for delays when you do your initial planning.*

Here are two worksheets and a checklist that will help you remember and schedule for the details that can derail you.

INFORMATION GATHERING: GET IT TOGETHER BEFORE YOU WRITE

Writing is like cooking; you have to have all your ingredients together before you can start. You don't want to discover that you lack a vital piece of information when you are already in the midst of writing. You can avoid this discouraging and unproductive situation by *planning your data gathering carefully* at the start.

DATA GATHERING WORKSHEET

Project: _____

Purpose of Project: _____

Reader or Readers: _____

1. What information do *I* need in order to write this?

(Note the type of information you'll need, e.g., test results, financial data, etc.)

2. What information does *my reader* need to understand it?

(Include any technical terms or abbreviations with which your reader might not be familiar.)

The following questions refer to the information that both you and your reader need.

3. Does this information exist now?

4. If not, what needs to be done to generate it? Do you need to request tests, credit checks, or some other kind of research? Who can generate this information for you? If you have to do it yourself, what steps are involved? Who can help you?

5. If the information already exists, where is it? Who has it?

There are many ways of getting information, including:

- Personal experience
- Asking questions
- Questionnaires and surveys
- Library research
- Database research
- Letters of inquiry
- Searching company records
- Site observation

Which of these will be most suitable to your task? What others might help you? Note specifically to whom you need to talk or where you need to look to find out what you need to know.

6. What obstacles do you think might block you from getting the data you need within the time you have available? How can you get around or eliminate these obstacles?

7. Before you launch into an extensive search for data, review your purpose, your main point, and your reader. Will this information fulfill your purpose, make your point, and touch your reader?

From *Get to the Point!* by Elizabeth Danziger, copyright © 2001 by Elizabeth Danziger (Three Rivers Press). This page may be photocopied for individual use only.

PROJECT SCHEDULING WORKSHEET

Project: _____

Starting Date: _____

Working Deadline: _____

"Killer" Deadline: _____

1. How many hours of *your* time do you figure this job will take?

   About how many hours per week will you need to spend on this project in order to complete it on time?

   Is it possible for you to realistically spend this number of hours on it in a week? If not, reconsider the deadline or scope of the task, or get someone to help you.

2. Do you need work fron the other people in order to finish this job? If so, how many hours of *other people's* time do you think it will take?

   Specify whose time you'll need and how much of that person's time you'll need.

Person: How many hours of this person's time do you need?

Person: Hours Needed:

Person: Hours Needed:

On the list below, note about how long you think it will take you to complete each phase of the writing. If it doesn't make sense to think in terms of hours, estimate in terms of minutes, days, or weeks.

From *Get to the Point!* by Elizabeth Danziger, copyright © 2001 by Elizabeth Danziger (Three Rivers Press). This page may be photocopied for individual use only.

PROJECT PLANNING CHECKLIST

I. GETTING READY

❑ Clarify the "Three P's": purpose, person, and point.

❑ Choose the best method of organization.

❑ Create an Organic Outline. (See pp. 54–61)

❑ Create a schedule, working backwards from your deadline to the present.

❑ Gather all your data.

II. WRITING

❑ Write a quick first draft.

❑ Sketch out any graphics. Send requests to graphics department.

III. REVISING

❑ Put it aside.

❑ Read it aloud.

❑ Make final graphics, or get proofs back from graphics staff.

❑ Revise it.

❑ Check final graphics.

❑ Submit full document to manager or client for review.

❑ Wait to get it back.

❑ Revise it again.

❑ Submit it to manager or client for final review.

❑ Wait to get it back.

❑ Make final revisions.

❑ Proof it until it's perfect.

IV. PRODUCTION AND DISTRIBUTION

❑ Send it out for binding or printing.

❑ Wait to get it back.

Review final version to ensure that the printer didn't
make some horrible mistake.

Send the document to its final destination.

This may mean shipping annual reports to a mailing house so that they
can mail them, or boxing a set of presentation handouts for shipment
to the client's office or hotel meeting room where your presentation
will be held. It could mean all kinds of things. Whatever your means of
delivering your finished product, the delivery process will take some
amount of time.

Don't let this last push catch you by surprise: Do everything in your
power to allow yourself an extra day for shipping and delivery, even if
you don't think you'll need it. The worst that can happen is that you
will look incredibly organized and efficient. The best that can happen
is that when the dispatcher for the overnight mail service mistakenly
puts your parcel in the "Second-Day Air" pile, you won't need to
panic.

TOTAL TIME YOU ESTIMATE YOU'LL NEED: _____

If this is more time than you have, look back over your esti-
mates and see where you might save some time. If you can't
shave off time without sacrificing quality, rethink the scope of
your project or the deadline. You may need to negotiate for
more time. On the other hand, you weren't really planning to
sleep for the next three weeks, were you?

From *Get to the Point!* by Elizabeth Danziger, copyright © 2001 by Elizabeth Danziger
(Three Rivers Press). This page may be photocopied for individual use only.

THE FIRST DRAFT: JUST DO IT!

The greatest mistake you can make in life is to continually fear that you will make one.
    —Ellen Hubbard

After you have planned your document and created your outline, one small step remains before you get on with revision: creating a first draft. By the end of the Organic Outlining process, you will have put your blocks of information in a logical order, verified that you have no redundancies or omissions, and written core sentences for each point. Completing these tasks at the outline stage will help you generate a stronger first draft than what you would have produced by writing a "grocery-list" outline. It will also be better than if you had done a brain dump onto paper and then tried to organize and edit your stream of consciousness.

From the Organic Outline, you can flow smoothly into your first draft. Look at your outlining surface as you begin to write. You have already written all of your topic sentences—they are on your sticky notes. You already have your paragraph groupings in a logical order. Your sets of major points with supporting points will become paragraphs. Now just write the sentences in the order you have put on your outlining surface.

You may want to reword some points or combine several short points into one sentence. As you write, you will find that some of the sentences seem too short and choppy. You can change the phrasing or combine related points into a longer sentence. It is easier to flesh out the phrasing or combine points than it is to edit out overwritten language. Here are a few additional points that will help you complete the first draft:

- The purpose of writing a first draft is to give you something to revise. Expect it to be imperfect. All first drafts are.

- Let the first draft flow out of you smoothly, even if you know it will need revision: Just get something on paper.

- Remember that no one need ever see this except you. You can throw it away or delete it if you want to.

- Write in a spirit of play, experimentation, and adventure. Demanding perfection at this stage will only make your creativity shrivel.

Part 4.
Dress Your Message for Success: Format Matters

You never get a second chance to make a first impression.
—Shoshana Lane

People do make snap judgments based on appearance. Maybe they shouldn't, but they do. They judge your written work by its looks, too. Make sure that your final letters and reports are dressed for success.

Rule 1: Keep it neat. Messy typing, crooked printing, smudgy pages, and lots of corrections give an impression of haste and carelessness. Sloppiness undermines your credibility and professional image.

Rule 2: Make it friendly. If your document is crammed with tiny single-spaced type, it will intimidate all but the most committed readers. Use subheads, bullets, and plenty of white space.

SUBHEADS REASSURE READERS

Imagine opening the morning newspaper and finding that it had no headlines—just columns of text with spaces in between. When you read the newspaper, you scan the headlines to get a sense of the day's news. Then you look more closely at the parts that interest you most. Given the chance, your readers want to do the same.

Use subheads and headlines liberally in letters, memos, and especially in reports and proposals. Summarize the main topic or point of your sections, sometimes even your paragraphs, by placing an underlined headline above them. Then a busy reader can get the feel of the document without having to pore over the whole thing.

PUT SPECIFIC INFORMATION INTO YOUR SUBHEADS

How helpful would it be if newspaper headlines said "International News," "Sports," "Opinion," and nothing more specific? You'd cancel your subscription pretty quickly. Give readers enough information in your subheads that your reader can follow your logic without reading every word of the text. Broad subheadings like the ones listed below may suggest categories to you but in your own work, write something specific, a brief, meaningful phrase—as the headline.

HEADLINE CATEGORIES YOU MIGHT USE

PROBLEM	PROPOSED SOLUTION
PURPOSE	CONCLUSIONS
FISCAL IMPACT	SUMMARY
ACTION REQUESTED	ACTION RECOMMENDED
EVALUATION	ENVIRONMENTAL IMPACT

Build on these general topic headings by adding a few words that describe the information which follows the headline. For example, you could write:

PROBLEM: Air-Conditioning Power Failures Cause Computers to Overheat

PROPOSED SOLUTION: Install Back-Up Generator in Computer Room

By giving the reader key facts in the subheads, you enable him or her to grasp the core ideas quickly. A subhead such as:

Fiscal Impact Will Be Minimal

is much more useful than one that simply says "Fiscal Impact." A subhead that says:

Immediate Sale of this Property is Recommended

is more helpful than one called "Recommendation." As always, put yourself in the reader's position: Don't you appreciate having a subhead that alerts you to the content of what you're about to read?

USE BULLETS WHEN YOU CAN

Bullet format enables your reader to take in several pieces of information at a glance rather than forcing him to plod through multiple lines of text. Imagine that these two documents contain identical information:

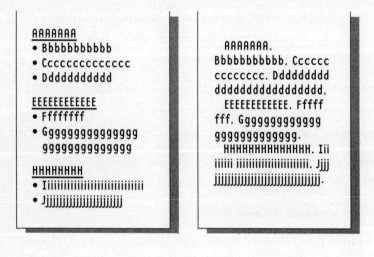

Which one would you rather read?

Sentences that contain many bits of data often work better in bullet format.

PUNCTUATING BULLETED SENTENCES

- If each bulleted item is a complete sentence, capitalize the first letter and put a period at the end.

- If each bullet point is a separate clause or phrase, you may put a semi-colon after each bulleted item. Then again, you may not. Putting semicolons between bullet points is a traditional usage that is slowly fading.

  - Some organizations still use the semicolon after each bullet point; some use a comma after each bullet point. Some companies don't punctuate at all after bullet points.

When deciding how to punctuate a bulleted sentence, let clarity be your guide. If the semi-colon after a bullet point is likely to help your reader understand the sentence, then use it. However, if the semi-colons add clutter and confusion to the page, then omit them.

No matter how you punctuate the end of each bullet point, your readers will be grateful to you for using bulleted format if your sentence contains a lot of data. For example, read this 50-word sentence in unbulleted form:

> Non-prime at 12/31/00 included $536m to remove an invoice included in the 12/31 aging that was originally billed and credited in December '00 and rebilled in January '01, $31m in accounts 90 days past due, and a $101m concentration reserve for account debtors in excess of a 25% concentration reserve.

Assuming that it is necessary to include all of this information in a single sentence, the pieces of information should be put onto separate lines using a bullet format. This gives the reader at least a remote chance of understanding the whole sentence at first reading.

> Non-prime at 12/31/00 included:
>
> - $536m to remove an invoice from the 12/31 aging that was billed and credited in December '00 and rebilled in January '01;
> - $31m in accounts 90 days past due, and
> - $101m concentration reserve for account debtors in excess of a 25% concentration reserve.

In an ideal universe, even this rewritten version could be streamlined. However, even an imperfect bulleted version is more intelligible than a 50-word behemoth.

WHITE SPACE RESTS THE EYE

Do you remember looking at library books in elementary school and trying to see whether they were "hard" or "easy"? Big letters, fat margins, maybe a few pictures—once you saw that there wasn't too much text on each page, you were in business. Your literary taste may have matured, but your eyes still enjoy white space. And why shouldn't they? Reading requires the tiny muscles around your eyes to keep your vision steady as you track tiny black marks across a perfectly straight line. Your eyes, and the muscles that hold your eyes on track, get tired. When they get tired, they need a little white space. They crave a space that contains no scratchy black letters. A place where they can blink, glance away from the page, and return smoothly to the task of reading. Give your readers a break: Allow ample white space on the page.

Which of these pages would you want to read first?

Your literary taste may have matured, but your eyes still enjoy white space. And why shouldn't they? Reading requires the tiny muscles around your eyes to keep your vision steady as you track little tiny scratchy black marks across a perfectly straight line. Your eyes, and the muscles that hold your eyes on track, get tired. When they get tired, they need a little white space. They crave a space that contains no scratchy black letters.

A place where they can blink, glance away from the page, and return smoothly to the task of reading. Give your readers a break: Allow ample white space on the page. Which of these pages would you want to read first?

White space rests the eye. It creates the impression that the page is easy to read. It gives the reader a natural place at which to look up from the page and makes it easier for him to find his place again when he resumes reading.

Don't sacrifice white space for the sake of skinny page margins. Allow a *minimum* one-inch margin on the top, bottom, right, and left of each page. If you must single-space the document, then skip a space between paragraphs so that the page will seem less dense.

Perhaps you had a teacher who told you to "get it all on one page." Like many other things this teacher told you, this is not entirely true. Make your message as concise and clear as possible. Cut the extra words and eliminate irrelevant points. If the document requires more than one page, then put it on more than one page. But don't cut out the white space.

Use white space liberally, even if it means that your final report will be a few pages longer. It is better to put your message on two pages than to cram it onto one page *that no one will read.*

Part 5.
STRUCTURE STRONG SENTENCES

Vibrant, clear language will move your reader and make him thrill to your words. Stodgy, tedious verbiage will make that same reader sigh and mutter, "Oh no! Not again!" before drifting away from your document into some more pleasant mental realm. No one sits down to write thinking, "I'm going to write the dullest letter my reader has ever read!" Yet many people do choose words that are more effective than melatonin at lulling readers to sleep. How can you avoid becoming your readers' best cure for insomnia?

It's simple: Write strong sentences. Choose the right words. Write with your reader in mind. Simple, but not easy. Here are some ideas to help you invigorate your writing.

SENTENCE BUILDERS: TEN WAYS TO SIMPLIFY YOUR SENTENCES

Making the simple complicated is commonplace; making the complicated simple, awesomely simple, that's creativity.
        —Charles Mingus

A sentence is a unit of thought. Before you can transmit your idea into your reader's mind, you must organize the idea into a sentence. Words won't do it: You can shower your reader with words all day long and not tell him anything. Only when placed into coherent sentences do your words become thoughts that are capable of appearing in the mind of another human being.

The word *sentence* comes from the Latin *sentire,* meaning *to feel.* The Latin word *sententia* means *opinion* or *decision.* The Latin *sententiosus* means *meaningful.* The English word *sentient* has the same root as *sentence*; it means *conscious,* having the power of perception by the senses. Thus, the concept of a *sentence* combines *feeling, judgment, and meaning.*

You have probably been told that "a sentence is a complete thought." This is true—within limits. Back in elementary school, when your longest thought was something like "When is recess?" or "What is the capital of Minnesota?" it was reasonable to define a single sentence as a single thought. However, you are now (I hope) dealing with more complicated thoughts. A complete thought may be composed of many sentences, each of which conveys one element of the thought. You don't have to cram your entire message between one capital letter and one period.

Research has proven that the most readable sentences are from 10 to 17 words long. If you want your readers to find your thoughts accessible and easy to retain, keep your average sentence length below 17 words. (Most word-processing programs enable you to find out quickly the average number of words per sentence in any document.) This does not mean that every sentence must be simplistic. Vary the cadence and rhythm of your sentences. A collection of "See Jane," "See Jane run" sentences are boring even for first-graders.

Every sentence need not be the same length, but your reader will be grateful if your *average* sentence length hovers around 15 words. For example, if your sentence contains a phrase like "generation-skipping estate transfer tax," you will be hard-pressed to get your point across in under 17 words. If one sentence is longer than 17 words, just be sure to use several short sentences (seven to ten words) in order to reduce your average. Remember: Lower average sentence length means greater readability.

In the next few pages, you will find tools to help you transform long, awkward sentences into sleek pieces of prose. These ten sentence builders will propel your ideas powerfully.

SENTENCE BUILDER #1. PUT THE ESSENTIAL IDEA INTO THE ESSENTIAL SENTENCE.

Every sentence has a **subject** and a **predicate.** The subject contains a noun and the words that describe the noun. The predicate contains the verb or action part of the sentence, along with the words that describe the verb. The grammatical core of every sentence is the subject-predicate combination. We will call this noun-verb combination the *essential sentence.*

For example, look at the sentence "He bought a Rolls Royce." The subject is *he*. The predicate is *bought a Rolls Royce*. The essential sentence is *He bought*. (A Rolls Royce is the direct object.) (If only it were as simple to do as it is to write!) We can add information to this sentence without altering the essential sentence. We could write:

> Because he had been out of town for ten of the previous
> twelve months and he realized that he had been neglecting
> his wife and children, he bought a Rolls Royce for them to
> use when driving to and from school.

Or we could write:

> After years of struggle and hard work, he bought a Rolls
> Royce so that he could drive around town in luxury and com-
> fort, pretending to ignore all the people who were pretend-
> ing not to stare at his car.

In the original version as well as the two different versions, the essential sentence is the same. Moreover, the essential *meaning* is also the same, regardless of his motivations, the fact remains that he bought the car.

The essential sentence should also convey the essence of your meaning. When you allow a gap to develop between the grammatical backbone of your sentence (the subject and predicate) and your basic idea, you weaken your writing and blur your message. For example, consider the sentence:

> It is amazing to me that he ever accumulated the money to
> buy a car at all, let alone a Rolls Royce.

The subject of this sentence is *it*. The predicate is *is*. Obviously, the sentence *it is* does not carry much information. True, the rest of the sentence tells the reader about the man and the car, but the strongest part of the sentence—the subject and the predicate—has been spent on words that say nothing about the essential message.

SENTENCE STRUCTURE 101

Before we look at the method for finding the essential sentence, here's a quick refresher of a few technical terms for parts of the sentence. Prepositions are connecting words such as *in, on, at, of, by, near, beside,* and many others. Prepositions are "anywhere a rat can run," as in "The rat ran under the refrigerator near the back door of our house by the sea." A prepositional phrase is just the group of words in which the preposition appears. So "under the refrigerator," "near the back door," "of our house," and "by the sea" are all prepositional phrases in the above sentence.

A dependent clause is a part of the sentence that *depends* on another part of the sentence in order to be meaningful. Dependent clauses are usually introduced with words like *which, that, since, because,* and others. Dependent clauses usually contain a noun and a verb, but they are not complete sentences because they are not meaningful on their own. For example, in the previous sentence, the dependent clause is *because they are not meaningful on their own.* This clause needs the remainder of the sentence or it doesn't make sense.

Now that we've quickly reviewed these terms, we move on to the technique for finding the essential sentence. (For more complete explanations of the parts of sentences, see page 134.)

FINDING THE ESSENTIAL SENTENCE

ORIGINAL SENTENCE:

Although you might believe that writing well is a skill reserved for people with unique talents, the fact of the matter is that you can probably write anything if you apply the ideas in this book.

1. Find all the *prepositional phrases* and draw a line through them.

Although you might believe that writing well is a skill reserved ~~for people with unique talents,~~ you can write anything if you apply the ideas ~~in this book~~.

2. Find all the *dependent clauses* and put brackets around them. (Marked in parentheses here.)

{Although you might believe that writing well is a skill reserved ~~for people with unique talents~~}, you can write almost anything {when you apply the ideas ~~in this book~~}.

3. Find and circle the *subject and predicate (action part)* of the sentence. (Marked in boxes here.)

{Although you might believe that writing well is a skill reserved ~~for people with unique talents~~}, you can write almost anything {when you apply the ideas ~~in this book~~}.

4. Now you can see that the essential sentence of this sentence is:

You can write.

*   *   *

Don't worry—you will not leave your essential sentences hanging naked on the page. In building your sentence, you're sure to insert dependent clauses and prepositional phrases. However, the essential sentence is your reference point, both in core structure and in core meaning. Knowing how to work with it will help you refine and strengthen your message.

FINDING THE ESSENTIAL SENTENCE HELPS YOU FIX YOUR SENTENCE STRUCTURE

Learning to spot the essential sentence will save you from many grammatical mistakes. Often, business writers make errors in a complex sentence that they would never make in a simpler sentence. They get confused in the midst of numerous phrases and clauses. Then they lose track of the subject and predicate of the sentence. Since all of the sentence's pronouns and verbs must match the subject and predicate, losing sight of the essential sentence is a costly error.

In the following examples, you will see how much easier it is to see mistakes in a singular-plural agreement and other basic structural points when you focus on the root structure of the sentence.

The Shipping department boxes and ships the items and confirm the shipment into the computer system.

Original Essential Sentence: The Shipping department boxes . . . ships . . . and confirm. . . .

When you look at this skeletal structure, you can see that the word *confirm* is incorrect. You would not write *The*

Shipping department confirm the shipment. But that is what this sentence says.

Corrected Essential Sentence: The Shipping department boxes . . . ships . . . and confirms. . . .

Having corrected the mistake at the level of the essential sentence, you can plug in the rest of the sentence to see the correct version:

Corrected Sentence →   The Shipping department boxes and ships the items and **confirms** the shipment into the computer system.

Here's another example:

Since cash and cash equivalents are combined on the balance sheet, the aforementioned transactions has no effect on the cash balance as a whole.

Although this sentence contains a lot of information, its grammatical subject is simply *transactions.* And the predicate? What action affects those transactions? As the sentence was originally written, the predicate is *has.* So the original essential sentence is:

. . . the transactions has . . .

When you look at the sentence in this simplified form, it is obvious that the sentence should not be *the transactions has.* Since *transactions* is plural, it requires the plural verb *have.* So the corrected essential sentence is:

. . . transactions have [no effect] . . .

Now you can replace all the original parts of the sentence and see the correct version:

> *Since cash and cash equivalents are combined on the balance sheet, the aforementioned transactions have no effect on the cash balance as a whole.*

Whenever you have a long or complex sentence to revise, begin by finding the essential sentence. The subject and predicate become your North Star, giving you a fixed point around which to correct and reconstruct the sentence.

SENTENCE BUILDER #2. USE THE ACTIVE VOICE.

> *If greeting card companies avoided the active voice:*
>
> *A Merry Christmas is wished to you . . .*
>
> *Sympathy is felt at your loss . . .*
>
> *You are loved by me.*

Verbs in the active voice tell the reader exactly who did what. Who hit the ball? The boy hit the ball. Who wrote the report? The manager wrote the report. Who decided to fire half the employees? The manager decided . . . Hey! Wait a minute! Does the manager really want to write, "The manager decided to fire half the employees"? He'd probably rather write, "It was decided that half the employees be fired." Therein lies the distinction between the active and the passive voice. Writers who want to be hazy about the true source of statements or conclusions often feel an overwhelming urge to slide into the passive voice. For example, these sentences are written in the passive voice:

> *It has been decided that no one will receive a Christmas bonus this year.*

Significant reduction of the number of employees on payroll
was determined to be the most appropriate course of action.

Who wants to be the Scrooge who stole Christmas? It's
so much simpler to use the passive voice. Unfortunately, pas-
sivity has a cost. The passive voice robs your work of energy
and aliveness and blurs your reader's sense of who is doing
what. It also makes your ideas more difficult to understand.

Here is a sentence set in the passive voice:

Prices are set by three in-house sales representatives on a
weekly basis from the respective current market prices of
the product less a 4% reserve.

Here's the same sentence, set in the active voice:

Three in-house sales representatives set the prices every
week. They base the price on the current market price of the
products less a 4% reserve.

The passive voice is formed with helping verbs such as
have, has, had, do, does, did, and so forth. It also lurks frequently in phrases that begin with *by.*

Look through your work and eliminate the forms "has
been [done]," "is [determined, done]", "was [sent, decided]"
whenever you can. Transform those wimpy passives into
forthright active verbs. If you have trouble recasting the sentence, just ask yourself, "Who is doing the main action here?"
Make that person or organization the subject of the sentence,
and voilà! You will be in the active voice. For example, compare:

Work will commence as soon as authorization is received.

to

We will begin work as soon as you authorize us to do so.

Or compare:

> *The completion of call reports by all salespersons should be mandatory.*

to

> *All salespersons must complete call reports.*

In addition to the fact that it weakens your writing, there is an ethical aspect to using the passive voice. The passive voice gives an impression that events just happened. Bonuses were cancelled. People were fired. At some level, the thoughtful reader wonders, "But *how* did it happen? Why did it happen? Who made it happen?" The passive voice is the written version of a writer shrugging her shoulders and saying, "Gosh, I don't know."

Your readers know that *someone* is *doing* the action described. They sense that it's a little slimy for that someone to hide behind the passive voice. Thus, relying too heavily on the passive voice eventually undermines your readers' trust. At some level, they are wondering what and why you are hiding. Does this mean that everyone will trust you if you use the active voice? No. But they will consider you a more straightforward person.

PROBLEM: Using the passive voice where you could have avoided it.	SOLUTION: Use the active whenever you reasonably can.
[x's] are denoted by [y's]	[y's] denote [x's]
[x] can be identified by [y]	[y] identifies [x]

WHO CARES WHO DID IT? WHEN YOU *SHOULD* USE THE PASSIVE VOICE

In a few situations, the passive voice is actually preferable to the active. Here they are:

1. You don't *know* who did the action.

The car had been vandalized.

2. You don't *care* who did the action.

Yankee Stadium was built in 19__.

3. Whoever did the action wants to remain anonymous or avoid responsibility.

A downsizing plan has been approved and will be put into effect shortly.

In short, although using the passive voice is generally a sign of weak writing, at times it is appropriate to use it.

Whenever you wish to steer the reader's focus away from the source of the action, describe that action in the passive voice.

SENTENCE BUILDER #3. WRITE WITH VERBS.

Verbs enliven language. They are your single greatest weapon against dullness. The higher the ratio of verbs to nouns, the more energetic your writing will be. If you add this one tool to your writing style—using more verbs—you will earn your readers' undying gratitude. Of course, nouns are necessary now and then, but when you begin to search for needless nouns in your work, you will find many that can profitably be rewritten as verbs.

Many unnecessary nouns lurk within words that end with *-ation, -ing, -tion, -ment, -ance, -al,* or *–ure.* Scrutinize words that end with *-ation* or *-ibility* and similar endings. Cross out the ending and ask yourself what verb you can form from this base. Use the verb instead of the noun.

THE (OFTEN) NEEDLESS NOUN	THE CRISP, ACTIVE VERB
determination	determine
give consideration	consider
proceed with the implementation	implement, do
attendance	attend
make allowances	allow
integration	integrate

TURN NEEDLESS NOUNS INTO VERBS

Another way to enliven your writing is to choose the verbal usage of words that can be used as either nouns or verbs. These words include *thought, use, need,* and *request.* Whenever possible, recast the sentence so that the same word functions as a verb. Compare these noun forms to the verb forms:

NOUN FORM	VERB FORM
Careful thought was given	We thought . . .
Return it after each use.	Return it after you use it.
As per your request . . .	As you requested . . .
Thank you for your call.	Thank you for calling.
Let's have a talk.	Let's talk.

The verbal form feels personal and immediate, while the noun form feels formal and distant. If you are striving for formality, you might choose the noun instead of the verb. However, if you want to express warmth and accessibility, the verbal form of the word will do it every time.

PROBLEM: Using nouns where you could have used verbs.	SOLUTION: Use the verbal form whenever you can.
[X] stated that payment would not be made.	[X] stated that he would not pay. Or [X] stated that [Y] would not pay.
[This event] is a representation of . . .	[This event] represents . . .
The inclusion of . . . [the reserve, etc.]	Including . . . [the reserve, etc.]
The issuance of [invoices, etc.]	Issuing [invoices, etc.]

SENTENCE BUILDER #4. PARALLELISM IS NOT A GYMNASTICS EVENT.

Parallelism is a writing technique that enables you to harness one of the most powerful needs in the human mind: the need to find patterns.

Using the same grammatical structure in a series of phrases is what makes the phrases parallel. In general, parallel phrases echo parallel ideas. A parallel sentence can be built around almost any phrase structure. For example, take

Julius Caesar's famous line: *I came. I saw. I conquered.* Each sentence has the same pattern:

pronoun	verb	pronoun	verb	pronoun	verb
I	came.	I	saw.	I	conquered.

Imagine that Caesar had written *I came. I saw. Gaul was conquered by me.* It wouldn't sound quite so imperial. The power of the original version is in its *parallelism* (and, of course, in the fact that he really did conquer Gaul).

The Bible is full of parallelism (as well as parables and parallels). For example, *a time to reap, a time to sow, a time to laugh, a time to cry. . . .* The rhythm of the passage rests on its parallel construction. Think of the same ideas expressed without parallelism: *a time to sow, harvest season, a time to laugh, and a time when a person feels like crying.* This kind of writing would probably not stay on the bestseller list for 2,000 years. Parallelism can apply to:

Words:

He is slow but thorough.

We are able to attract, retain, and motivate the most talented employees.

Phrases:

Her routine was always the same: First she went to the pool, then she went to the beauty parlor, and then she went to the club.

Dependent clauses:

> I'm calling about the book that you borrowed two years ago,
> and which you promised to return promptly.

Prepositions:

> "The character of a company is a matter of importance to
> those in it, to those who do business with it, and to those
> who are considering joining it." (Sir Adrian Cadbury)

Independent clauses:

> But, in a larger sense, we cannot dedicate—we cannot con-
> secrate—we cannot hallow this ground. (Abraham Lincoln,
> "The Gettysburg Address")

Using parallel construction for ideas is a basic element of an emphatic, vigorous writing style. Witness the sentence below, from the first chapter of Jack Kerouac's *On the Road*. Here Kerouac is introducing Dean Moriarty, a main character.

> He can back a car forty miles an hour into a tight
> squeeze and stop at the wall, jump out, race among
> fenders, leap into another car, circle it fifty miles an
> hour in a narrow space, back swiftly into a tight spot,
> jump, snap the car with the emergency so that you see
> it bounce as he flies out; then clear to the ticket
> shack, sprinting like a track star, hand a ticket, leap
> into a newly arrived car before the owner's half out,
> leap literally under him as he steps out, start the car
> with the door flapping, and roar off to the next avail-
> able spot.

Notice the sense of motion Kerouac creates by establishing a pattern of short, vivid verbs: ". . . back a car, stop . . . jump . . . race . . . leap . . . circle . . . back . . . jump, snap . . . clear. . . ." His description of Moriarty dashing around a parking lot may leave you breathless.

SENTENCE BUILDER #5. DON'T DANGLE YOUR MODIFIERS.

Fried in fat-free oil, you can feel good about eating this chicken.

"Avoid dangling modifiers." The first time I heard this advice, I tried to envision what a dangling modifier must look like. It sounded like a hazard in a construction zone. Like you, I asked myself, "What *is* a modifier anyway?" And I found out: A modifier is a word or group of words that alters (i.e., modifies) the meaning of a word or sentence. We say that a modifier is *dangling* when it is not clear exactly what it is supposed to be modifying. For example, take the sentence:

While reading the newspaper, the dog got loose.

The modifier is *while reading the newspaper*. The problem is that we don't know for sure who was reading the newspaper. Was it a person or a dog? If you had written

While I was reading the newspaper, the dog got loose.

no one would steal your dog for use in animal-literacy experiments. Splurge on the few extra words that make your meaning clear.

REPAIRING THE DANGLING MODIFIER

If you suspect that you've written a dangling modifier, how do you fix it?

1. Identify the essential sentence (core noun and verb).

This will make it easier to find the dangling modifier.

2. Identify the intended or implied subject of the phrase.

3. Add the missing subject to the main clause.

Rearrange the sentence as necessary, putting the phrase as close as possible to the noun it relates to.

Here are a few examples of dangling modifiers and their solutions.

After listening to his presentation, his plan became clear.

This implies that the plan listened to the presentation. The question is "Who actually listened to the presentation?" If it was you, then write,

After I listened to his presentation, his plan became clear.

Here's another:

By going on vacation, our credit card debt doubled.

This implies that your credit card took a cruise. But we know that credit cards don't take cruises; people do. Credit cards just make it easy for people who go on cruises to spend lots of money. What really happened was that

After we went on vacation, our credit card debt doubled.

And another example:

Unless signed and dated, no employees may turn in expense reimbursement forms.

Most employees would not take kindly to being signed and dated. In order to avoid confusion (and perhaps mutiny), write

Employees may not turn in expense reimbursement forms unless the forms are signed and dated.

(Note: It is better to repeat the word *forms* than to leave the meaning unclear.)

SENTENCE BUILDER #6. BEWARE THE PREPOSITION TRAP.

Prepositions connect pieces of information in sentences with amazing agility. Therein lie both their strength and their weakness. They are so handy that they enable writers to compose gems like this:

Consolidated accounts receivable totaled $22,232M with $1677M or 7.4% in excess of 90 days from invoice date compared to accounts receivable totaling $19,333M with $1,135M or 5.8% in excess of 90 days from invoice date at 12/31/00.

This sentence is part of a work sample submitted by a participant in one of our writing workshops. (He wrote it *before* he took the class.) The prepositions in the offending sentence are *with, in, of, from, to, with, or, in, of, from, at.* That's 11 prepositions. Remember that the optimal average length for a sentence is from 10 to 17 words. Woops. When people end up with sentences so long and convoluted that even their writers cannot remember their original idea, prepositional phrases are often the culprits.

There are two reasons why it is dangerous to use too many prepositions in a sentence.

1. Grammatically, prepositions are weak.

The strong parts of your sentences are the subject and the predicate. Yet it is very tempting to keep on stuffing information into the sentence with words like *of*, *in*, and *at*. The danger is that you will put an important piece of information into a phrase that is grammatically insignificant. This raises the likelihood that the reader will scoot past it without realizing its importance.

Prepositions are so handy that they may lull you into composing sentences that are too long.

3. Prepositions entice writers into making basic grammar errors.

The vase of flowers are on the table.

The subject of this sentence is *vase*; it requires the singular verb *is*, yet it is painfully easy to look at the plural *flowers* and write *are*. If a sentence contains several prepositional phrases, it is easy to lose track of the grammatical subject of the sentence and become confused about whether to use a singular or plural verb. For example:

Due to higher returns and lower prices of computers, the gross profit for computer systems have also dropped to 5%.

The subject of this sentence is *profit*—a singular noun. Yet the writer has put the verb *have* as the predicate. This leaves an essential sentence that reads *"Profit have [dropped]."* Matching the singular word *profit* to its correct verb would give us this essential sentence:

Gross profit for computer systems has also dropped.

Prepositions are like sugar; it is easy to sprinkle them on everything, but they don't necessarily improve the finished product.

SENTENCE BUILDER #7. BREAK SENTENCES AT CONJUNCTIONS.

If you want to take apart a long sentence, cut it at the seams. Simple sentences are impossible to cut because they're seamless! Complex or compound (read *l-o-n-g*) sentences are stitched together by connecting an independent clause to a dependent clause using a relative pronoun (like *which, that, since,* or *because*) or by connecting two shorter sentences with a conjunction, a "joining" word (like *and* or *but*). The simplest way to shorten a long sentence is to:

• Break at conjunctions that separate two independent clauses.

The easiest place to cut a long sentence is at a conjunction. The conjunction is the fulcrum point between two independent clauses, so it is the place where two shorter sentences are connected.

They went to the movies and then they went out to dinner.

Then went to the movies.   They went out to dinner.

- Break at relative pronouns that separate an independent clause from a dependent one.

He finally bought the car that he'd been longing for.

He finally bought the car.   He'd been longing for it.

Words like *which*, *that*, *since*, and *because* are natural spots at which to break apart a sentence.

DON'T GO ON AND ON

"Where shall I begin, please Your Majesty?" he asked. "Begin at the beginning," the King said, gravely, "and go on till the end. Then stop."

— Lewis Carroll, *Alice's Adventures in Wonderland*

Did you hear about the new support group for people who can't stop talking? It's called *Anonanonanon*. When members of this group start writing, they tend to write sentences that go on and on and on—also known as run-on sentences. You can create run-on sentences in two ways:

- By sticking what should be two sentences together with a comma, a conjunction, or with nothing.
- By combining several related clauses into one behemoth that is too long for your reader to comprehend.

For example:

We went to the store and we saw the cars driving outside in the street and at home Johnny was watching TV.

Mrs. Wilson, our neighbor, is a snoop, she is always looking out her window when we come home at night.

If you're not sure whether you have a run-on, read the sentence aloud and listen for the points where your voice intuitively pauses or stops. These are the places where you're likely to have omitted a period or comma. Insert a period at the point when your voice stops or naturally inflects downward. Here's the secret to avoiding run-on sentences: when it's time to stop, stop!

SENTENCE BUILDER #8. STATE POINTS POSITIVELY.

We are not retreating—we are advancing in another direction.
  —General Douglas MacArthur

When my son was four years old, I retrieved my telephone messages and heard the following message from his preschool teacher: "It's not an emergency—we're just wondering if Michael is up to date on his tetanus shots." I thought a rabid squirrel must have bitten him. As it happened, he had only been bitten by a mad toddler. What a relief.

People want to know what *is,* not what isn't. The moment you begin a sentence with "It's not . . ." or "Although . . ." or "Please don't think . . . ," your reader has divided his attention in half and is anxiously anticipating disaster. If it's *not* X, then what on earth *is* it? Unless you have good reason to create suspense, don't do it. Just tell the person what's so. The classic negative phrasing is:

"There is nothing to be alarmed about."

You reassure your reader more by writing:

"We have a small problem, but we can handle it."

Another example:

The change in net profits resulted not so much from a decline in sales as from an increase in overhead expenses.

Better to write:

Increased overhead expenses led to the decline in net profits. Sales did not decline significantly.

Tell your reader what *is*. He can figure out what isn't.

SENTENCE BUILDER #9. REDUCE REDUNDANCY.

Every unnecessary word that you add to your text will subtract from your reader's attention. Repeating the same idea within a sentence will not add to its impact. More likely, it will only annoy the reader. Using two words that have the same meaning will not make your idea doubly meaningful. So don't repeat yourself.

When revising your work, read each sentence ruthlessly: Have you used the same *word* several times? Have you repeated the same *idea* more than once? Hunt down repetitions and delete them.

Don't squander the time your reader is willing to share by inflicting redundant phrases like these:

plan in advance (Did you ever try to plan in retrospect?)

resume again (What does *resume* mean?)

reduce down (What does *reduce* mean?)

pending receivables (Aren't all receivables pending?)

little miniatures (Unlike those giant miniatures)

advance reservations ("I want a reservation on last Friday's flight.")

one A.M. in the morning (One A.M. *is* one in the morning.)

round in shape

young in age

small in size

return back

SENTENCE BUILDER #10. CREATE VIVID IMAGES.

What was the happiest moment of your life?

Did your memory of that moment come to you in words? Or was it an image—looking at your spouse on the day of your wedding, seeing your newborn child's face for the first time, shaking the dean's hand when you received a hard-earned diploma?

Visual images pack emotional power. They spur readers to action and engrave memories in the mind. You structure your thoughts with general statements, but you bring those thoughts to life in your reader's mind when you illustrate them with vivid images. How can you paint more pictures in your readers' minds?

Include the details. We live our lives in physical details, and in those details our memories are stored. Can you see the

way your mother held her fork as she ate? Hear the sound of
your sibling breathing as you slept side by side? Feel the satis-
fying heft of the football as you launched your first touch-
down pass? Smell the salty breeze as you first stood by the
sea? Taste the ice cream in your mouth on the hottest day of
summer? Each detail releases a cascade of related memories
and sensations.

Sensory verbs and images anchor your message. The
more clearly you can paint an image in your reader's mind,
the more completely he or she will remember your message.
What kinds of words create mental images? Words that contain or allude to color, movement, sound, and touch. In contrast, weak verbs connect different parts of a sentence without
provoking a sense of vitality. For example, notice the heart-
pounding intensity triggered by a statement like:

> There is a problem with the customer service department,
> and we should do something about it.

Compare that to

> Our customer service representatives often interrupt, con-
> tradict, belittle, and berate our customers. This behavior
> will no longer be tolerated. Representatives who fail to
> uphold our standards will be fired.

Combining specific details and strong verbs clarifies the
picture. Compare, for example, the non-specific statement:

> If you lack adequate life insurance, your family might suffer
> after you are gone.

to the detail-filled visualization:

> How would your family live if you were to die tomorrow? How
> long could they pay the mortgage before they had to face
> foreclosure? Could they continue to live comfortably? Could
> your son keep taking guitar lessons? Could your daughter
> get those braces she needs? And what about college? Losing
> you would be tragic enough—don't compound your family's
> loss by leaving them without ample life insurance.

People remember pictures. Each descriptive verb strengthens the reader's mental picture. When you give specific details, using powerful verbs, you create a clear image in your reader's mind. True, adding visual details may increase your word count. However, what you are aiming for is impact and memorability. Too many of the wrong words will dull your impact and make your reader long for amnesia. But the right words will penetrate the heart and mind and leave a vivid imprint there.

Remember the power of the image. Link strong images to your key thoughts. A picture may be worth a thousand words, but it doesn't take a thousand words to create a mental picture.

SENTENCE BUILDERS: TEN WAYS TO SIMPLIFY YOUR SENTENCES

Sentence Builder #1. Put the Essential Idea into the Essential Sentence.

Sentence Builder #2. Use the Active Voice.

Sentence Builder #3. Write with Verbs.

Sentence Builder #4. Parallelism is Not a Gymnastics Event.

Sentence Builder #5. Don't Dangle Your Modifiers.

Sentence Builder #6. Beware the Preposition Trap.

Sentence Builder #7. Break Sentences at Conjunctions.

Sentence Builder #8. State Points Positively.

Sentence Builder #9. Reduce Redundancy.

Sentence Builder #10. Create Vivid Images.

Part 6.

CHOOSE WORDS WISELY

Your words are like arrows that carry your meaning to your reader. Some words are strong while others are flimsy. Some are armed with poisoned tips while others carry harmless suction cups. Some are new and fresh while others have been shot across the archery course so many times that they're about ready for the firewood pile. The work you've put into structuring your document will help you aim your message accurately, but you've got to choose the right words to carry your ideas. Even if your aim is perfect, choosing weak or ambiguous words is like shooting a plastic arrow with a suction cup tip. Flimsy "arrows" will not penetrate the mind of a thick-skinned reader.

The strongest words you can choose are verbs. Verbs add life and movement; nouns just sit there. Increase the ratio of verbs to nouns in all your writing, and your writing will come alive.

TO BE OR NOT TO BE? NOT

You can use connecting or "linking" verbs such as *be, do,* and *have* in almost any sentence. This should alert you to the fact that they are frequently the coward's choice in terms of vocabulary.

Sometimes you must use these verbs, especially when defining terms or stating a location. If you are using the verb as an equal sign, as in *Today is Thursday* or *He is an American,* then you are using *is* correctly in its basic linking function. Go ahead and write "The cat is on the mat" (if it is) or "The woman is short" (if she is). But beware of overusing *is,* lest it lead you into verbosity and put your reader to sleep.

When tempted to use *is* and *be,* remember this: If your sentence states that something exists, then use *is* or *be* or *are. He is Tarzan. We are the champions. Will you be there?* However, if you want to describe any aspect of the subject's existence more clearly, then find a verb that creates a more specific image.

Leaning on *is.*	Using a *real verb.*
How is it different?	How does it differ?
He is not very often on time.	He usually arrives late.
It is the lowest paid, least motivated group of employees that has the most frequent interaction with customers.	The lowest paid, least motivated group of employees interacts most frequently with customers.

WHAT IS, IS

Despite its weakness as a descriptive term, the verb *to be* does have one significant benefit. Variations of *to be* are quite useful when you are trying to seem profound. Even an ordinary or nonsensical thought sounds deep if you keep referring to *being*. Watch this:

Being is being. What is the is-ness of being? Being is.

And just remember, folks: Everything is everything.

USE STRONG, VIVID VERBS

Good writing is supposed to evoke sensation in the reader—not the fact that it's raining but the feel of being rained upon.
            —E.L. Doctorow

Colorful, vibrant verbs produce writing that is persuasive, dynamic, and specific. They energize and uplift your writing. A strong verb evokes imagery and movement. In contrast, a weak verb seems vague or lethargic. Compare these sets of weak and strong verbs:

WEAK: go

STRONG: stride, stroll, swagger, limp, pounce, amble, gallop, dash, waltz

WEAK: say

STRONG: cajole, shriek, shout, declare, whisper, announce, stutter, bellow

WEAK: do

STRONG: accomplish, behave, practice, produce, solve, suffice, manufacture

Strong verbs create vivid pictures. They increase the sense of force and individuality of the document. They provoke more interest and spark more curiosity. When you catch yourself lapsing into ho-hum verb choices like *do, go,* and *say,* pause and ask yourself, "What do I really mean? How can I be more specific?" Pepper your writing with powerful verbs and people will focus more fully when they read your work.

"ALL MY LIFE I'VE ALWAYS WANTED TO BE SOMEBODY—MAYBE I SHOULD HAVE BEEN MORE SPECIFIC."

—Jane Wagner, *The Search for Signs of Intelligent Life in the Universe*

Words like *more, better, some, less,* and *soon* enable us to seem assertive without actually asking for what we want. If you write an internal memo asking that your department devote "more resources to this project," the manager could send you a box of pencils and say that he fulfilled your request.

If you tell your secretary, "You must do better if you want to keep your job," he has no way of knowing what you mean by *better.* Is his typing inaccurate? Does he revise your work too freely? Is he rude to clients on the phone? Does he make the coffee too strong?

If you inform a key customer that his order will be shipped "soon," will he feel confident about your firm and your service?

When you find yourself slipping into more-dom, ask yourself whether vagueness truly serves your purpose. You might find that:

1. You are not sure what you want.

Take the time to clarify your request in your mind before verbalizing it.

2. You don't have enough information to make a specific request.

Try to get the relevant information.

3. You must be vague in order to protect your *derrière*.

This is a judgment call. Will ambiguous language benefit you in the end?

4. You are afraid that if you ask for what you want, you will make your reader angry—and still not get what you want.

If you think your request will annoy your reader, then explain your reasoning briefly before making the request. If you are sure that your request will anger your reader, why are you making it?

The next time you are inclined to write "please return this to me as soon as possible," pause before you write. Do you really need it back by Friday at 5:00 P.M.? Tell the person what you mean. If "please return it by 5:00 P.M." seems curt, then soften the request. You could write, "I would really appreciate it if you could get this back to me by 5:00 P.M. today."

It's been said that the problem with American culture is its preoccupation with having *more*. Maybe we ought to be more specific.

YOU JUST GO—THROUGH THE RAPIDS

When my son was 13, his class went on a river-rafting trip. As I drove him to meet his group, he said, "This is so stupid! Do you know that there has to be a guide in every boat?!" I said I thought it was a good idea to have someone on the boat who'd done it before. True to his age, he scoffed, "But it's easy. I'm sure I could do it myself."

"Really? How would you do it?"

"You just go—through the rapids."

"Just go"—it sounds so simple before you fall in the water.

Broad general terms are useful shorthand for describing things or processes that would otherwise require reams of explanation. It's appropriate that we should use broad strokes for many descriptions. However, as we draw those strokes, we should remember how much detail, passion, life, and pain are packed into them. You might read about someone who inherited a modest sum and then "parlayed" it into a huge fortune. Or a person who had one hamburger stand and then "built" it into a multinational restaurant empire. Decades of difficulties are blithely compressed into *parlayed* and *built*.

Use general terms to introduce specifics and to summarize—but be careful not to trivialize the living experience that is packed into them.

AVOID LEGALESE AND GOBBLEDYGOOK

Unless you are a lawyer, you'll find that highly legalistic terms are rarely essential. And words like *hereinafter* and *whomso-*

ever could probably vanish from the language with no legal consequence at all. Using legalese identifies you as a stiff, highly formal individual, when in reality you are a warm, friendly, terrific person. So why give the wrong impression? Even lawyers are trying to sound less like lawyers when they write. Don't adopt their bad habits just as they're trying to give them up.

Gobbledygook is stuffy formalized language. Writers often use it because they think they have to write like this in order to have credibility. If you are writing to very stuffy, formal people, this is probably true. Get out there and utilize the nomenclature mentioned hereinafter. However, if you want to cultivate a friendlier tone and remove linguistic roadblocks between you and your reader, take Ernest Hemingway's advice: "Eschew the monumental."

PLAIN AND SIMPLE	STUFFY AND FORMAL
use	usage
used	utilized
begin	initiate or commence
but	nevertheless
tell	advise
get or buy	procure
expect	anticipate
get	obtain
expensive	economically prohibitive
end or fire	terminate

about	pertaining to
before	prior to
nevertheless	notwithstanding the foregoing

Use legal language when you are dealing with a legal issue in which you may be held liable for *not* using a specific legal term. Otherwise, leave the gobbledygook to the turkeys.

The beginning of wisdom is to call things by their right names.
    —Chinese proverb

PASSIVE *IN SITU* BIO-REMEDIATION: AVOID JARGON

Jargon is technical language that relates to a particular professional group. These professional buzzwords are great when you are writing to a colleague, but they are deadly in work that will be read by anyone else. "Passive *in situ* bio-remediation" is a technical term that means letting something sit outside until it rots. The Latin term does sound classier than "letting it rot." Is it jargon? It depends. If your reader would understand it and it fits within the tone of the document, then bio-remediation is not jargon. If you have left a priceless piece of equipment out on the yard and it's rusted beyond redemption, then you should definitely call it *in situ* bio-remediation and pray that your boss flunked Latin. But if you are writing for ordinary people and you want them to understand you, then use regular words. By *regular*, I mean words that you might find in *USA Today* or a local newspaper. You know, *regular*.

PROBLEM: Using long words or phrases when a short one would do.	SOLUTION: Use the shorter version of the same concept.
is comprised of	consists of
[X] is primarily dependent on [y].	[X] depends on [y].
on a weekly basis	every week/weekly
on a daily basis	every day/daily
as such . . .	What does this phrase mean? Consequently? Therefore? Thus? Whatever you do mean, write it. "As such" doesn't say much.
respectively . . .	Avoid using this word. Instead, clearly separate the two sets of items you wish to compare.

ACRONYMS R A-OK?

Acronyms are brief and easy to remember. They look cool when embroidered onto baseball caps. Even better, they save you from having to write "National Aeronautics and Space Administration" or "American Federation of Television and Radio Artists" over and over again. They are also great ways of avoiding calling things by their real names. Acronyms turn terms that might sound gross, disgusting, or scary into chipper little bits of lingo.

The military establishment and the nuclear power industry are great fans of acronyms. For example, *LOCA* stands for "Loss of Coolant Accident." If it happens in your car, it's an inconvenience; in a nuclear power plant, it's a meltdown.

A disadvantage of using acronyms is that the same acronym can have wildly divergent meanings. AMA is the acronym for American Medical Association, American Management Association, Australian Medical Association, Academy of Model Aeronautics, American Motorcycle Association, Adaptive Management Area, American Marketing Association, and dozens of other groups. If you blithely drop "AMA" into your document without giving the reader some major clues about the context, you're likely to confuse someone. Remember to define the acronym the first time you use it in a document. To you, it might be obvious that NRA stands for Neurological Rehabilitation Association; still, you might as well clarify it before you start getting hate mail addressed to Charlton Heston.

CLICHÉS ARE FOR DWEEBS

A cliché is a trite, worn-out phrase that was exciting when it was coined but has since been used so often that everyone is tired of reading it. Many English clichés have their origins in the Bible and classical mythology or in the works of pithy writers like William Shakespeare and Benjamin Franklin. Wherever these phrases came from, however, they came a long time ago. Rather than taking the easy way out and using a phrase that you've already read dozens of times, *replace clichés with new metaphors or choose simple, clear words that say what you mean.*

Another reason to avoid clichés is to avoid the embarrassment that comes from finding out that a term you've been blithely using for years actually has a sad or off-color connotation. For example, "Sweets to the sweet" comes from a speech by Shakespeare in which Hamlet throws flowers on top of the drowned corpse of Ophelia, who has just committed suicide because of her unrequited love for him. Says Hamlet, "Sweets to the sweet, farewell." Think about that the next time you hand someone a box of candy and say "sweets to the sweet."

TRENDY OR TRITE?

Elegance is refusal.
        —Coco Chanel

Trendy words sound new and up-to-date. People use them to demonstrate that they are hip to what's cool. Occasionally, these words survive for a few years and become useful additions to society. Sometimes, they thrive for a while and then linger as parasites on the linguistic consciousness of the world. Words like

per

Per John's memo, we're going to change the policy.

interface

> When attending a party, it is important to interface with all
> the single women.

and *implement*

> I have a strategy for taking out the garbage, but I haven't
> implemented it yet.

have the distinction of going directly from being trendy and overused to being boring, trite, and overused. In general, trendy words are like sushi: They are only good when they're fresh.

The life cycle of trendy words is becoming shorter as information moves ever more rapidly around the world. Even words like *cyber* and *virtual* are starting to sound old, and millions of people still haven't figured out what they mean! Using trendy words is like playing a pyramid scheme. It's fine while you're passing it on to the next unwitting user, but woe to the chump who is still saying *groovy* after everyone else has moved on to *awesome*! The fickleness of linguistic fashion is yet another sound reason to avoid trendyisms entirely. Remember, basics never go out of style.

OMIT NEEDLESS WORDS

This report, by its very length, defends itself against the risk of being read.

    —Winston Churchill

CHOOSE WORDS WISELY   119

If you want your writing to be more brief, you have to use fewer words. The artistry lies in knowing which words to use and which ones to lose. The following tools will help you oust the enemies of brevity.

USE SHORT, FAMILIAR WORDS

Short words are best. Old short words are best of all.
        —Winston Churchill

Recall a time you were reading and came to a word whose meaning you didn't know. What did you do?

A. Go scampering off to the dictionary to use this opportunity to increase your word power?

B. Try to figure out the meaning of the word from the context and then proceed on the assumption that your guess was right?

C. Think, "What a snob! Why can't he use ordinary words?" and throw away the document?

Most readers opt for B or C. If they guess the meaning, there's a chance that they will guess wrong and therefore miss your point. If they throw away your document in disgust, it's even less likely that they'll grasp your message. So if you want your readers to be receptive and understanding, use words that they know: Use short, familiar words.

Short words are usually words of Anglo-Saxon origin or root words descended from Greek or Latin. Root words are not cluttered with *prefixes* and *suffixes*. A prefix is a group of letters that goes before the root of a word, and a suffix is a group that comes after the root.*

Some prefixes are:

pre-	post-
extra-	inter-
intra-	anti-

Some suffixes are:

-ability	-ation
-ness	-ance
-ization	-ology

Avoid gluing prefixes and suffixes to otherwise innocent words. Your writing will be stronger and clearer if you resist this urge. Use strong verbs and uncluttered everyday nouns. You'll be amazed at the impact you can make. Consider the following passage from the biblical book of Ecclesiastes:

> *I returned and saw under the sun, that the race is not to the swift, nor the battle to the strong, neither yet bread to the wise, nor yet riches to men of understanding, nor yet favor to men of skill; but time and chance happeneth to them all.*

What images and feelings does this passage evoke?

* For a comprehensive list of Greek and Latin prefixes, suffixes, and roots, see pages 247–55.

Now read the following paragraph, written by George Orwell to paraphrase the original biblical passage using words of Greek and Latin origin:

> Objective consideration of contemporary phenomena compels the conclusion that success or failure in competitive activities exhibits no tendency to be commensurate with innate capacity, but that a considerable element of the unpredictable must invariably be taken into account.

Which version would you pick up for inspiration?

DOWN WITH *PER*

Per is a Latin word. For those of you who speak Latin as a second language, it means *through, throughout, of, at, by means of, under pretense of, for the sake of.*

People often use *per* as though it were an English word meaning *according to* or *as.* However, the problem is that *per* does not mean either *according to* or *as,* and even if it did, you would be better off writing in English than in Latin.

So please: No more *per*!

NEVER QUALIFY AN ABSOLUTE

"Will you please play with me?" he asked.

"Certainly not," said the lamb. "In the first place, I cannot get into your pen . . . In the second place, I am not interested in pigs. Pigs mean less than nothing to me."

*"What do you mean, **less** than nothing?" replied Wilbur. "I don't think there is any such thing as **less** than nothing. Nothing is absolutely the limit of nothingness. It's the lowest you can go. It's the end of the line. How can something be less than nothing? If there were something that was less than nothing, then nothing would not be nothing, it would be something—even though it's just a very little bit of something. But if nothing is **nothing**, then nothing has nothing that is less than **it** is."*

"Oh, be quiet!" said the lamb. "Go play by yourself! I don't play with pigs."

—E.B. White, *Charlotte's Web*

The original meaning of the word *absolute* is *undiluted* or *pure*. If you dilute the meaning of the absolute term, then it's not an absolute anymore. A qualifier is a term that places some limiting condition on the word that follows it. A qualified success is a project that turned out well despite drawbacks. An unqualified success was good by any measure.

By definition, an absolute is unqualified. If it were qualified, it wouldn't be an absolute. For example, the word *maximum* means *the highest possible point.* Either the point you're describing is the highest or it is not. If it is, then it is the maximum; if it is not, then it is not the maximum. If you write that your production capacity has reached its absolute maximum, including the word *absolute* does not add new information. If the capacity is at its maximum, then we already know that it has reached its limit. Adding words like *absolute, complete,* and *total* to words that are absolute terms in themselves actually diminishes the reader's sense that you are confident of your statement.

Here are a few common phrases that load unnecessary qualifiers to words that were fine as they were.

complete stop

absolutely nothing

totally empty

100% pure

exactly equal

absolute minimum

absolute maximum

completely full

MAKE YOURSELF UNPOPULAR! USE THESE PHRASES

Old phrases never die. They just become part of the boiler-plate language in large organizations. I would like to ask that you carefully survey the standard text in your organization for the purpose of obliterating these flabby phrases:

we would like to ask that you

for the reason that

are of the opinion that

for the purpose of

subsequent to

with respect to

during the course of

succeed in making

at this point in time

ABOLISH *RESPECTIVELY*!

The word *respectively* sends this message to the reader: "I, the writer, did not care to take the time to sort out the information I'm trying to convey to you, so I am going to jumble it all into one sentence and let you sort it out." This is rude. The onus is on the writer (that's you!) to organize the facts and separate them into understandable packets of information.

DIS-RESPECTIVELY SPEAKING

With *respectively*

Inventory turnover for the periods ended 12/31/92 and 12/31/93 was consistent at 178 and 170 days, respectively.

Without *respectively*

Inventory turnover was consistent: turnover for the period ended 12/31/92 was 178 days, while turnover for the period ended 12/31/93 was 170 days.

DON'T HEDGE

Words such as rather, pretty, very, and little are the leeches that infest the body of prose, sucking the blood of words. We should all try to do a little better, we should all be very watchful of this rule, for it is a rather important one and we are pretty sure to violate it now and then.

—E.B. White

Don't fatten up your work by hedging your points with namby-pamby modifiers. If your goal is to make your point clearly, why clutter it up with words like *very* and *seemingly*? Notice as you read whether they really add anything to your comprehension, other than an uncomfortable sense that the writer is protesting too much. Avoid hedging by avoiding the following:

rather

seemingly

somewhat

kind of

mostly

very

pretty

little

it would seem

in some respects

for the most part

for all intents and purposes

What is wrong with hedges and modifiers? They block your points. They consume the reader's time and energy on words that add nothing to your message.

AVOID EMPTY INTRODUCTIONS

The truth of the matter is that more often than not, it seems to me that people often tack empty introductions onto their points. Unfortunately, vacuous introductory phrases are more likely to annoy than to placate your reader. Even worse, these phrases imply that you are insecure or uncertain of your point.

Avoid introductory phrases like these:

the truth is that

it seems to me

apparently

it is obvious that

as I recall

the fact is that

I also want to say that

as a matter of fact

and all their meaningless cousins.

A brief introduction sets the stage for your statement. However, phrases like *the truth is* or *the fact is* actually cast doubt on your sincerity. If your statement is true, state it firmly and the facts ring true. Phrases like *it seems to me* or *I also want to point out* are downright annoying. If you are writing the document, the reader assumes that you are writing as it seems to you.

"SEE YOU AT WHITSUNTIDE!"

As Americans, we have an annoying habit of acting as though our country, our holidays, our customs, and our language are meaningful and important to everyone else in the world. It is foolish—and often offensive—to be ethnocentric when the entire planet is just a keystroke away.

We may blithely assume that our customer in Taiwan is hip to Halloween but then be shocked when we call someone in Japan and find out that they're having a national holiday on a day when *we* are working. Stumbling over another nation's holidays is not a good way to gain entrance into the global economy.

If you are referring to a uniquely American holiday like Thanksgiving or Halloween, either say that this date is a holiday or omit any reference to it. If you are shipping an item overseas and expect it to arrive in late November, don't write, "you will have it around Thanksgiving." Tell them to expect it in late November. What would you think if a British company promised to ship an item to you "around Whitsuntide"?

REFER TO PEOPLE

Everything you write about boils down to something that *somebody* did. Referring to the people who worked, studied, built, assessed, moved, and so forth adds life to your writing. People read your reports, and they know that you, a person, wrote those reports. Don't pretend to be an abstraction.

Referring to people will warm up the tone of your writing because it will force you to shift from the third person (*he, she, it*) into the first or second person (*I, you, we*). Third-person pronouns like *he, she,* and *it* create formality and distance. Words like *you, we,* and *I* build the reader's sense of connection with you.

REMEMBER THE MAGIC WORDS

We cannot always oblige; but we can always speak obligingly.
        —Voltaire

Courtesy and consideration are as essential in memos and letters as they are in conversations—perhaps even more important because the reader can note their absence every time he looks at the page. Do not edit etiquette out of your work. Use those magic words *Please, Thank you, I'd appreciate it, I'm sorry*. Courtesy is appropriate in every document.

WARM IT UP

Tone describes the feeling or emotion that the reader is left with after reading a piece of writing. A cool tone is formal and stiff, while a warm tone is informal and friendly. Just as vocal tone conveys a tremendous amount of information to the listener, far beyond the literal meaning of the words, so does the tone of your writing convey countless subtle messages about you and your attitude toward your reader.

Latin- and Greek-based words generally convey a more formal tone. Using the passive voice creates an even more distant tone. Imagine receiving an invitation like this:

Please attend our domicile-warming on August 5.

If you decided to attend, you would not expect a casual down-home housewarming.

Short, Anglo-Saxon words written in fairly short sentences using casual punctuation (such as dashes) convey a breezy, informal tone:

We hope you can be there—the get-together is on August 5.

If you are not sure whether the tone of your work is warm or cool, read the document aloud. You will hear how your words are likely to sound to the other person; this will enable you to judge whether the tone you have adopted really suits your relationship with that person.

MAKE YOUR POINT AND GET OUT

I never saw a person who could cram so small an idea into so many words.
        —Abraham Lincoln

When you belabor points that you've already made, you lose your impact.

We've all had the experience of making our point—and then making it, and making it, and making it, and making it again. When we do this in person, we see our listener's eyes gradually glaze over as he or she begins contemplating the best way to end the conversation.

When we do it in writing, though, we don't see our reader gradually become frustrated, lose interest, and finally throw away the document that we labored so long to prepare. As writers, we have less control over our readers' "round-file power" than we do when we are speaking.

WRITE FOR YOUR READER, NOT FOR YOURSELF

If you want to write in a way that pleases yourself, that's fine. Write whatever you want. Just don't expect anyone else to read it. If you want your readers to read and understand you, however, you'll have to keep their interests in mind. And what is most interesting to most people is themselves. Remember the inner questions your reader is asking himself as he reads your document: *Why me? What am I supposed to do about it?*

Sometimes you may show the reader what benefits he will get from paying attention to what you wrote. Other times you need to tell him what you want from him, that is, what he needs to *do* because of reading what you wrote. You might even need to point out the hazards of not attending to your message. The sooner you show your reader that you've thought of his needs, the happier your reader will be. Remember:

- Quickly point out the benefits of reading your work.
- Make your format visually appealing.

- Write only when you have something to say.
- Show the reader that you have taken his interests and needs into consideration.
- Get to the point as soon as possible, so that you don't waste your reader's time.

Your reader will reward you with his attention.

Part 7.

HELP FOR THE GRAMMAR PHOBIC

Grammar is to a writer what anatomy is to a sculptor, or the scales to a musician. You may loathe it, it may bore you, but nothing will replace it, and once mastered it will support you like a rock.
—B.J. Chute

Quick—what comes to mind when you think of grammar? Diagramming sentences? Memorizing conjugations? Somehow, the word *grammar* does not conjure images of joyous creativity. Yet without grammar, no creative writing would be possible. In fact, no boring writing would be possible either. No writing at all is possible without grammar because grammar gives order and consistency to language. Grammatical rules are the core set of agreements on which a language is built. At times you may bend the rules if it will help your reader understand you. Over time, grammar may even change. When it changes, however, it changes slowly as a growing consensus of readers and writers adapt the language to their evolving usage of the language. Even if it becomes acceptable to start a sentence with *but* or to end a sentence with a preposition, there will always be grammar.

Participants in my writing seminars often agonize over grammar and punctuation: "Did I use the semicolon right?"

they ask. "What's the rule about the final apostrophe?" These are important questions because they show that these people care about getting their ideas across and that they don't want to look like idiots to the people they work with. If your writing contains mistakes in grammar and punctuation, your reader may doubt your competence and intelligence.

It is vital to know basic grammar and punctuation. However, (and this is a big however), the fundamental purpose of language is *not* to avoid all grammatical errors. It is to *convey meaning*. The rules of grammar and punctuation matter primarily because they enable us to convey meaning to our readers more precisely. If you meticulously follow the rules of grammar yet leave your reader befuddled about your meaning, then you have not written successfully. If bending the rules is the best way to get your meaning across, then bend them. All I ask is that you know what rule you're bending.

PARTS OF SPEECH

There are eight parts of speech in English: *nouns, pronouns, adjectives, verbs, adverbs, prepositions, conjunctions,* and *interjections.* (If you remember all the parts of speech, then skip this section.)

NOUNS

The noun fills the space in:

Jim's chocolate _____* is really delicious.

* cake

Nouns are names. Nouns may name people, things, places, or concepts. They can be concrete, as in *candy, pen, steps;* or they can be abstract, as in *faith, hope,* and *charity.*

Common nouns are general terms such as *man, house,* and *dog.*

Proper nouns are specific terms for particular members of a group, for example, *Mr. Jones, the White House,* and *Fido.*

PRONOUNS
The pronoun fills the space in:

_____* loves to eat chocolate cake!

Pronouns substitute for nouns and other pronouns. Pronouns are divided into three groups, which are known as *cases:* the nominative, the objective, and the possessive. (You don't really have to know those terms but it might be fun to bandy them about someday to show that you're in the know.)

PRONOUN FORM	WHEN TO USE THIS FORM	EXAMPLE
Nominative	Use when the pronoun is part of the subject of the sentence.	*We came home.*
Objective	Use when the pronoun refers to the object of a verb or preposition.	*John came home to see us.*
Possessive	Shows ownership or possession	*John came to our house.*

* He

Here are the most common English pronouns, in all their forms:

NOMINATIVE	OBJECTIVE	POSSESSIVE
I/we	me/us	my/ours
you	you/you	yours/yours
he/they	him/them	his/theirs
she/they	her/them	hers/theirs
it/they	it/them	its/theirs

VERBS

The verb fills the spaces in:

Jim's chocolate cake _____* really delicious. Or "He _____** chocolate cake."

Verbs express action. They also place actions in time: present, past, or future. Verbs may express action or condition.

*is   ("Is" functions here as a linking verb; it acts like an = sign.)

** loves to eat   (These words together form the action of the sentence; this phrase is also known as a predicate.)

ACTIVE VERBS CARRY CLOUT

Verbs place actions in time: present, past, or future. Verbs may express action or condition. For example:

He ate a fish. (Action)

He was a fish. (Being)

Sometimes verbs simply link what comes before them with what comes after them. When they do this, they are called *linking verbs.* The verb *be,* in all its forms, is the most common linking verb.

ADJECTIVES

The adjective fills the space in:

Jim's _____* cake is _____*.

Adjectives modify nouns or pronouns. They describe or limit these words, giving the reader a more exact sense of the writer's meaning. For example, a *delicious* meal, a *disgusting* meal, or worse yet, an *expensive, disgusting* meal.

Adjectives answer the questions: "Which one?" "What kind?" "How many?" "Whose?"

Sometimes pronouns function as adjectives. Words such as *my, his, her, its, our, your, their, mine, yours, myself, yourself,* etc. can also be considered adjectives, depending on their context.

  * chocolate   * delicious

ADVERBS

The adverb fills the space in:

Jim's chocolate cake is _____* delicious.

Adverbs modify verbs, adjectives, other adverbs, or clauses. Adverbs often express time, place or direction, manner, degree, or assertion.

* unusually

PREPOSITIONS

The preposition fills the space in:

Jim brought the chocolate cake _____* the company party.

A *preposition* is a word that connects a noun or a pronoun with another word in a sentence and makes clear the relationship between the two. A "prepositional phrase" is simply a group of words that contains a preposition and its object. For example, *on* is a preposition; *on the desk* is a prepositional phrase.

* to

CONJUNCTIONS

The conjunction fills the space in:

Jim _____* his coworkers ate the whole thing.

Conjunctions join words or groups of words. Some conjunctions link words or groups of words that are of the same order or rank. These include *and, but, for, nor, or, yet.* Other conjunctions link subordinate clauses to main clauses. These include *as, as long as, often, before, since, when, while, because, since, although, if, unless, whether, so that, in order that, than.* Conjunctions are often used in pairs, as in *both . . . and, either . . . or, so . . . as,* etc.

* and

INTERJECTIONS

The interjection fills the space in:

_____* ! That cake was great!

Interjections express emotion. For example, *Oh! So! Welcome! Bang! Oh dear!* (*Wow!* That cake cake had 1,000 calories per serving!) You probably will not use many of them in your business correspondence.

* Wow

THE ONLY SENTENCE PARTS THAT MATTER

A sentence is a group of words that expresses a thought. Single words can express an image or a concept, but only a sentence can convey a thought. You can think of a sentence as having only two elements: *the essential sentence* and *the extra information.* The essential sentence contains the subject and the predicate. Everything else is extra. (As mentioned in Part 5, the essential sentence is the ideal starting point for any sentence revision.) There are many technical terms to describe the basics and the extras, but it will help you to keep this basic distinction in mind.

The **subject** of a sentence is the person, object, or idea being described. Subjects are nouns, pronouns, or phrases used as nouns. The *essential subject* is the one word—usually a noun—upon which the whole subject is based.

The index of this book is useful.

Index is the essential subject; *index of this book* is the complete subject.

His party attracted many people's attention.

Party is the essential subject; *his party* is the complete subject.

Sally's new computer lost its cookies.

Computer is the essential subject; *Sally's new computer* is the complete subject.

The **predicate** is the action, condition, or effect of the subject. It's the part of the sentence that tells you what happened. Predicates are verbs and the words used to explain the action or condition. The *essential predicate* is the one verb (with or without a helping verb) that relates directly to the essential subject.

The index of this book is useful.

Is is the verb; *is useful* is the predicate.

His party attracted many people's attention.

Attracted is the verb; *attracted many people's attention* is the predicate.

Sally's new computer lost its cookies.

Lost is the verb; *lost its cookies* is the predicate.

Those two parts, the subject and the predicate, form the backbone of every sentence. Without them, you have no sentence. That's why we call them the "essential sentence."

WHAT IS A SENTENCE MADE OF?

Another way of looking at sentences is to say that they consist of one or more *clauses*. Let's look at the two major types of clauses.

TYPES OF CLAUSES

A clause is a group of words containing a subject and a verb. There are two types of clauses. ***Independent clauses express a complete grammatical thought and can stand by themselves.***

I run.

He and she run together.

Dependent or subordinate clauses do not express a complete grammatical thought, though they may have a subject and a verb. They cannot stand alone. Dependent clauses establish a relationship between two thoughts. Like phrases, dependent clauses are hanging or subordinate sentence parts. If you are not sure whether a clause is dependent, read it aloud. Dependent clauses sound incomplete, while independent clauses sound complete. For example, we might write:

The stock market crashed. Many people lost their fortunes.

Both of these statements are independent. To show a relationship between these two thoughts, you might write, *When the stock market crashed, many people lost their fortunes.* Here, the phrase "when the stock market crashed" is the subordinate or dependent clause. *Many people lost their fortunes* remains independent.

You could also combine the first two sentences into: *The stock market crashed, which means that many people lost their fortunes.*

In this example, *the stock market crashed* remains independent, while *many people lost their fortunes* becomes part of the dependent clause.

You can decide whether to emphasize a piece of information by placing it in the primary, independent position in the sentence, or whether to subordinate it into a clause beginning with *which, that, since,* or *because.*

DIRECT OBJECT

Actions, and therefore action verbs, usually have *objects.* Someone or something feels the result of the action described by the verb, so it is called the object of the verb.

> The dog bit *the man.* (The man is the object of the bite.)

> He threw *the vase* on the floor. (The vase is the object of violence.)

> The room contained *a hundred people.* (The people are receiving the action of containing.)

You can figure out the object of a verb by asking "What?" or "for whom?" after the action. The dog bit whom? The man.

CAPITAL OFFENSE

Nouns follow a caste system: There are common nouns and proper nouns. (The proper nouns never invite the common nouns over for tea.) Only the proper nouns are capitalized.

Capital is Latin for head; thus, words that go at the head of sentences or that represent a particular individual get a capital letter. With words like dog or Snoopy, deciding whether to capitalize the noun is a no-brainer. However, business writers often struggle when trying to decide whether to capitalize the "s" in *southern California* or the "f" in *federal law*. The following points will resolve some common questions about capitalization:

1. Always capitalize proper nouns.

Proper nouns describe a unique member of a general group. For example, your manager is only one of thousands of managers (although he may not believe it). So it would be pretentious to write, "My Manager suggested I write to you." Similarly, there are countless presidents, chairmen, and other big shots on this big planet. They only rate a capital letter when their title is connected to their name (and even then the capital might be superfluous). For example, Abe Lincoln was introduced as President Abraham Lincoln before he gave the Gettysburg Address. But the next day's newspapers would have read, "The president spoke briefly."

In short, words like *manager, committee, county, firm, president,* and the like are not proper nouns unless they appear as part of a specific name.

2. Don't make it a federal case.

Which is correct: "Don't make a Federal case out of it!" or "Don't make a federal case out of it!"? The *Chicago Manual of Style* states that the full names of government bodies should be capitalized but that *adjectives* derived from those names should be lowercased. For example,

Many people feel that the federal government has too much power. However, laws such as the Federal Emergency Management Act have been helpful to millions of people.

City Councilman Fred Jones declared, "We can no longer allow these scofflaws to avoid paying business tax. In fact, according to Municipal Code 123, the penalties for failure to pay city business tax can be quite severe."

3. Don't imagine that you will make something seem More Important by capitalizing it.

Capitalizing for emphasis falls into the same category as double underlining, boldfacing, spouting exclamation marks, and other visual tricks that are supposed to tell the reader how thrilled and impressed he should be with what you've written. If your point is important, put it in a sentence structure worthy of its significance. Don't rely on cheap tricks to help hammer home your message. When it comes to capitals, less is More.

4. Follow your organization's standards, even if you think they are wrong.

Different industries, organizations, and managers have different customs regarding capitalization. Most of them use too many capital letters. However, you can only complain about a certain number of policies before you begin to sound like a nag. Do you want to exhaust everyone's patience by insisting that Vice President should not be capitalized? Wait for the really important issues—such as when you are going to get a raise.

Unless you are prepared to be a lonely maverick—or unless you're the boss—go along with the style preferences of your organization. As long as you're not lowercasing people's names, the worst that can happen is that you will use too many capital letters. This is bad, but not as bad as being unemployed.

5. If you are unsure about whether to capitalize, *don't*.

The general trend among professional writers is to capitalize less. Retain the capital letters at the beginning of sentences. Keep the ones at the beginning of a name.

SOUTHERN OR SOUTHERN?

Words like *north, south, east,* and *west* pose special challenges for concerned writers. We all know that North America gets a capital North, and South Dakota gets a capital South. But what if you are going to New Zealand and you want to ask someone in what direction the water drains in the southern hemisphere? Is it the southern hemisphere or the Southern Hemisphere? Travel agents are likely to capitalize the hemisphere because it is bound to be more expensive to travel to a place that is capitalized than it is to go somewhere that is not capitalized. (And water drains counterclockwise when you're that far south.)

And what if you are going on vacation in Arizona, New Mexico, and Utah? Are you visiting the southwest or the Southwest? Or is it the southwestern United States or the

Southwestern United States? It's almost enough to make you want to stay home.

Even staying home wouldn't save us from questions about company names. If you work for the company that provides natural gas to the southern portion of Arizona, then whom do you work for? Southern Arizona Gas? Or southern Arizona Gas?

Unfortunately, there is no definitive answer to these troubling questions. When the word is not part of the proper noun, it should be capitalized for clarity or for emphasis. If you mean only to convey the place where your vacation is taking place, you can say you're going to visit the southwest (as long as your reader knows what country or states you are referring to). But if you want your friends to be prepared for you to return wearing boots, chaps, and a sombrero, you'd better warn them that you're going to visit the Southwest. Similarly, if you are an art dealer representing artists from New Mexico, you will certainly want to say that you are a dealer in Southwestern Art. Who wants to pay those prices for southwestern art?

PRONOUNS: JUST BETWEEN WE

"... even Stigand, the patriotic archbishop of Canterbury, found it advisable—"

"Found what?" said the Duck.

"Found it," the Mouse replied rather crossly: "of course you know what 'it' means."

"I know what 'it' means well enough, when I find a thing," said the Duck: "it's generally a frog or a worm. The question is, what did the archbishop find?"
—Lewis Carroll, *Alice's Adventures in Wonderland*

Pronouns substitute for nouns and other pronouns. These handy little stand-ins prevent us from having to write something like *Sue brought Sue's dog to Sue's cooking class, and Sue's teacher became angry at Sue.*

When the pronoun is part of the subject of the sentence, use the nominative case: *I went to see Martha.* When the pronoun is part of the object of the sentence, i.e., the recipient or object of the action described, then use the pronoun in the objective case: *Martha came to see* **me**. When you want to indicate possession, use possessive pronouns, as in *Martha came to see* **my** *piano.*

Obviously, using these words is not brain surgery. However, confusion often prevails about the pronouns *me* and *us*. Somewhere in recent history, it became uncool to say "me." Maybe it was when Cookie Monster began growling, "Me want cookie!" Whatever the reason, the fact is that *me* and its plural partner *us* have gotten a bad rap. Both of these pronouns go in the place of the *object* of a phrase or preposition. For example, *between* is a preposition. So if you want to say *between you and* _____, what is the correct pronoun? Right! It's *me*. Contrary to the beliefs of certain broadcast personalities, there is nothing classy about saying or writing *between you and I.* Maybe we should keep that just between us.

IT'S ABOUT ITS

The company reported that it's third quarter sales were down.

The Post Office is raising it's rates.

The committee issued it's report.

Has the world lost its mind? Or it's mind? Or it's mind's? People seem to be muddling the use of the words *its* and *it's* with distressing frequency. The confusion about the distinction between *its* and *it's* springs from the fact that *it's* looks suspiciously like a word that might have two meanings. Unfortunately, it doesn't. It means one thing only: *it is*. *Its* also has only one meaning: *belonging to it*. This distinction is generally covered in elementary school, but many people seem to be suffering from repressed memory syndrome on this point.

Here is where *its/it's* confusion may originate. The possessive form of **nouns** is formed by adding an apostrophe-s ending.

It is Mary's book.

That is John's car.

The company's earnings are up.

However, the possessive form of **pronouns** is *not* formed with an apostrophe:

The book is hers.

That is his car.

Its earnings are up.

Logic might dictate that nouns and pronouns should form their plurals the same way, but grammar says otherwise.

There is never an apostrophe-s ending in a possessive pronoun. Most people know this instinctively—except when dealing with the word *its*.

Its means *belonging to it*. As in, *The house has a chimney. Its chimney is red.* Just as you would not write *hi's car*, or *that one is her's*, **do not write** *The Post Office took it's time* or the like.

It's is the contraction of the phrase *it is*. The apostrophe shows where a letter has been omitted. For example, instead of *he is*, we write *he's*. Instead of *is not*, we write *isn't*. And instead of *it is*, we write *it's*. If you are ever unsure whether to use *it's* or *its*, separate the *it* from the *is* and you'll know what to do. For example, if you are tempted to write

> The company reported that it's third quarter sales were down.

note that this really means

> The company reported that it is third quarter sales were down.

which is clearly nonsense. If you want to write

> The club is raising it's dues.

note that what you are really saying is

> The club is raising it is dues.

In these two examples, the right word is *its*. *Its* means *belonging to it*—whatever *it* is.

A small thing, you might say. An apostrophe here or there, what's the difference? But carelessness about detail is insidious. If we write one thing when we mean another, we betray the primary function of language. There is enough ambiguity of every sort afoot in our world. Let's keep our language clear.

AND ABOUT YOUR ANTECEDENTS

Remember that pronouns are only stand-ins for nouns. Before you use a pronoun, you have to tell your reader what it refers to. If your reader ends up wondering what your pronoun refers to, then the pronoun is worse than meaningless: It is confusing.

Words like *he, she,* or *it* could refer to any one of millions of people or things. Pronouns are only useful if your reader can easily answer the questions "Which *he?* What *she?* What *it?*" because there are a whole lot of *he's, she's* and *it's* out there to choose from. The technical term for the noun to which the pronoun refers is *antecedent.* For example,

Susan said that she saw Jim at the party.

The antecedent is *Susan;* the pronoun is *she.*

After Harry called Jill, she went to pick him up.

Harry is the antecedent of *him. Jill* is the antecedent of *she.*

John brought his mother the bread that he had baked for her.

John relates to *his* and *he. Mother* relates to *her.*

When pronoun reference is clear, readers won't notice it. They'll just understand the sentence and get on with their lives. When the reference is unclear, however, they get confused. Shortly after they get confused, they start to get annoyed. Let's not think about what happens after that. Here are a few examples of sentences with ambiguous pronoun reference:

After John told Bill about the problem, he wished that they
had talked about it sooner.

Who wished that they had talked about it sooner? John or
Bill?

Jill brought her mother the bread she had baked for her.

Who baked the bread? Probably it was Jill . . . but based on
the information in this sentence, it could have been Mom,
too. Don't make your reader guess.

GENERAL POINTS ABOUT PRONOUNS

Follow these general rules, and you'll avoid trouble:

- Place the pronoun as close as possible to its antecedent.
- Avoid placing the pronoun where it may refer to more
than one antecedent.
- If you think the reader might be confused about what
you're referring to when you use *it, this,* or other pronouns,
then repeat the noun. Even if your sentence sounds clunky,
it will fulfill its primary function, which is to get your message across.

ANYWHERE A RAT CAN RUN

Contrary to what Miss Grindle may have told you in the fifth
grade, you will not die from ending a sentence with a preposition. However, if you entangle your readers with too many
prepositions, you may lose their attention.

A preposition is "anywhere a rat can run." (The only exception to this is *of*.) For example, a rat can run:

about, above, across, after, against, along, among, around, before, behind, below, beneath, beside, between, beyond, by, down, during, except, for, from, in, into, like, off, over, through, toward, under, until

And all of these are prepositions.

As Miss Grindle undoubtedly told you, it is *generally* not a good idea to end a sentence with a preposition—unless it is. If your sentence reads more gracefully or is more understandable with the preposition at the end, then put the preposition at the end.

An apocryphal story about Winston Churchill may clarify this point. Sir Winston sent a draft of a speech to a subordinate for review. This fellow sent his boss a memo noting that the speech contained a sentence that ended with a preposition and suggesting that the sentence be changed. Churchill shot back a note saying, "This is the kind of nonsense up with which I will not put."

ARE YOU SINGLE?

Many words are grammatically singular even though they seem to refer to a plural. I know this isn't fair, but hey, life isn't fair. Words like *staff, team, company, group, committee,* and *board* obviously conjure up images of groups of people. Yet it would be a mistake to write *The staff are going to hate this* or *The*

Board of Directors are going on a retreat. Why? Because these words are singular, and they require singular verbs. The singular-plural issue offers one of those refreshing moments in life when the difference between right and wrong is still clear: Singular nouns take singular verbs, and plural nouns take plural verbs. Period.

Pronouns that **feel** plural but **are** singular are another source of singular-plural confusion. The following pronouns are singular: *each, everyone, everybody, anyone, anybody, someone, somebody, no one, nobody, one, many a one, another, anything, either, neither*.

Notice that these singular words often contain the word *one* or *body*—reminding you that the word refers to one body—a singular one, we presume.

THE ERROR OF PROXIMITY: TOO CLOSE FOR COMFORT

The Grammar Police have a term to describe what happens when an unwary writer uses a verb that matches the word that is *closest* to it rather than the word to which it really refers. They call it the "error of proximity." This grammatical principle follows the well-known life principle that we tend to follow the behavior of those closest to us, even when we shouldn't.

Consider the statement *a vase of flowers is on the table*. The subject of the sentence is *vase*. If you were just describing the location of the vase, you would certainly write *the vase is on the table*, because you know that the singular noun *vase* requires the singular verb *is*. However, once you put flowers

154 GET TO THE POINT!

into the vase, you create the possibility of confusion. The subject of the sentence is still *vase*; the flowers are a grammatical detail, no matter how central to the room décor they may be. Nevertheless, many unwary writers have written *the vase of flowers are on the table* because the plural word *flowers* is next to (that is, in immediate proximity to) the verb.

If you wish to avoid the error of proximity, remember this: If your subject is plural, then your verb must be plural. If your subject is singular, all the verbs you use to refer to it in a given sentence must also be singular.

Writers often trip over prepositions when trying to sort out whether a verb should be singular or plural. Therefore, pay special attention to sentences containing prepositions when you check your work for correctness. For example:

The entire group of aviators are going to the convention.

Knock out the prepositional phrase *of aviators* and you see that the essential sentence is *The group are going,* which is wrong.

In short, proximity is a good thing, but only among elements that are compatible.

PROBLEM: Mismatched singular-plural references.	SOLUTION: Maintain agreement between singular and plural.
each [of the accounts] . . . were	Each [of the accounts] was
The major assumptions used in the study was . . .	The major assumptions used in the study were . . .

COULD EVERYONE BRING THEIR OWN MONEY?

For thousands of years, in dozens of cultures, the word *he* was understood to refer in certain contexts to both men and women. Similarly, the word *man* is often understood to refer to mankind or humanity, depending on the context. Readers understood that *everyone will bring his own money* meant that women would still be expected to buy their own drinks.

However, many women have come to resent being casually lumped together into the same pronoun with all those Y-chromosome carriers. They clamored for gender-neutral language. Rather than make any sexist assumptions, the gender-neutral writer would write *everyone will bring his or her own money.* While this usage solves the problem of assuming that *him* automatically includes *her,* it creates a different problem: The use of *his or her* and the like is incredibly tedious. It makes sentence structure more complex and strikes many readers as faintly ridiculous. This is why many writers resorted to the gender-free pronouns *they/their* in their quest for linguistic emancipation. So we traversed the distance from

Everyone brought his own money.

to

Everyone brought his or her own money.

to

Everyone brought their own money.

which was a little silly, since in every case, women still had to buy their own drinks. Moreover, *everyone brought their own money* led to what seemed to be a fundamental grammatical error. It matched the singular pronoun *everyone* to the plural pronoun *their*. This is against one of the Top Ten Commandments of Good Writing: "Thou shalt not match a singular noun to a plural pronoun or verb." (Maybe it's in the Top Twenty or Thirty Commandments, but it is right up there.)

For people who care deeply about getting grammar right, and about the integrity of the language, and about the growing laziness, imprecision, and spineless ambiguity that permeates public discourse everywhere, every variant of *everyone brought their own anything* is a painful reminder of everything that is wrong with America today.

These singular-plural mismatches can usually be corrected in one of two ways:

1. Make the subject of the sentence plural and thereby avoid the problem altogether. So you might rewrite the offending sentence as *All of the guests brought their own money.*
2. Recast the sentence so that it doesn't use personal pronouns at all, as in *Everyone brought money.*

Cognitive psychologist Steven Pinker suggests an interesting justification of the *everyone brought their own money* usage in his book, *The Language Instinct.* Pinker writes that when ordinary people read a sentence like *Everyone returned to their seats,* they know that the sentence means that everyone who had a seat returned to it. He has a linguistic rationale for all this, which is thoroughly explained in his book (but not in my book). Suffice it to say that in Pinker's view, there is a grammatical justification for writing *Everyone brought their own money.* And Dr. Pinker is a very smart fellow. Does that mean that you should start propagating sentences about everyone doing their own thing, or being their own person, or whatever? Not necessarily. Making the whole sentence plural, or depersonalizing it altogether, is still the more prudent choice. But then, everyone has their own opinion on this topic.

AVOID ADVERB ABUSE

Verbs tell us what happened in a sentence; adverbs tell us the juicy details. For example, suppose that Fred and Agnes left the party together. That's interesting, but *how* did they leave? Furtively? Proudly? Angrily? Quickly? Early? Adverbs clue us in. They describe verbs, adjectives, other adverbs, or clauses.

Adverbs express time, place or direction, manner, degree, or assertion. Here are some samples:

Manner: *slowly, quickly, always, often, once, twice*

Degree: *too, very, entirely, much, little, almost* (Note: In a phrase like "the sooner the better," *the* is not an adjective; it is known as an *adverb of degree*.)

Assertion: *yes, no, surely, possibly, truly, perhaps, probably*

Time: *again, often, then, now, soon, today*

Place or direction: *here, there, above, below, away, down*

Adverbs are moveable beasts. Unlike adjectives, they can be dropped into a sentence almost anywhere without changing the meaning of the sentence. For example,

The firemen ran up the stairs.

Up the stairs ran the firemen.

Either way, you know where the firemen went. You could even write

The firemen ran swiftly up the stairs

or

Up the stairs the firemen ran swiftly.

Adverbs are the only parts of speech that can be picked up and dropped with such ease. In fact, one way to test whether a phrase contains an adverb is to see if it could be placed elsewhere in the sentence without any loss of meaning.

Adverbs can be great friends as long as you don't get too chummy with them. For example, if you write, *They ran swiftly down the street*, you have a decent sentence. However, if you find that you're packing multiple adverbs and adverbial phrases into a sentence, consider making it into two sentences or restructuring the sentence.

ADVERBS WITH AN ATTITUDE

Instead of describing an action, adverbs sometimes describe the writer's *attitude* about the sentence at hand. When placed at the beginning of a sentence, adverbs like *admittedly, alarmingly, basically, generally, honestly, ideally, incidentally, predictably, supposedly, hopefully, fortuitously, unfortunately, inexplicably, understandably,* and their ilk tell us the flavor of the sentence that follows. These adverbs do not necessarily refer to a particular verb within the sentence; rather, they tell us about the writer's frame of mind.

DON'T KILL THAT WHICH!

Many people mistakenly believe that they can shorten their sentences by eliminating words like *that* and *which*. They may not realize that by deleting these words, they wipe out their reader's sole clue to the relationship between the first half and the second half of their sentence. Shortening a sentence by removing these relative pronouns is like cleaning up a highway by removing all the traffic signs. The road is tidier, but drivers and pedestrians don't know where they are. For example, take the sentence:

> *The main reason for the change in the turnover was the shipping season in Florida is usually a month ahead of the western region.*

The sentence leaves the reader in doubt. Did the turnover change because of the shipping season in Florida? Or was it because the shipping season happens sooner in Florida than it does in the west? There is no way to know for sure without a relative pronoun. Imagine the reader's sigh of relief upon reading

> *The main reason for the change in the turnover was **that** the shipping season in Florida is usually a month ahead of the western region*

Here's a sentence that could benefit from the inclusion of a few which's:

> *This device is not only a cell phone but also a powerful palm pilot device combining telecommunicating and web browsing and including the capacity to perform diverse wireless functions.*

Notice how the ideas in the sentence seem to fall all over each other and leave you puzzled about what the writer is talking about. In the following version, *which's* have been wedged between the ideas to help you keep them separate:

> This device is not only a cell phone but is also a powerful palm pilot device **which combines** telecommunicating and web browsing and **which is capable of** performing diverse wireless functions.

You still might not want to buy the device, but at least you have a better idea of what it does.

If you see too many *which's* in your sentences, the solution is **not** to kill the which. All those *which's* should be whispering in your ear that your sentence is too long. Splurge! Write several sentences instead of one long one. Choose a few *which* clauses and elevate them to the rank of independent clauses by deleting the relating word (*which, that, because, since*). Tinker with what's left over until it can stand alone. Turn your one long sentence into several shorter ones. Then those scary *which's* won't bother you anymore.

WHO IS THAT WHICH?

Many years ago, an editor called me discuss revisions of an article I had written. He said casually, "Shall we go with the standard usage of *which* and *that?*" Nonchalantly I replied, "Sure." As I said this, I was thinking frantically, "What *is* the standard usage?" I have since been gratified to learn that millions of people are as confused as I was. I have also learned that there are in fact two schools of thought about the proper use of these relative pronouns: the Just-Do-It approach and the Grammar Police approach.

THE JUST-DO-IT APPROACH

Which should be used to refer to things only. *That* may be used to refer to both things and people. *Who* refers only to people.

This software, which I told you not to buy, is not compatible with our mainframe.

Please return the book that you borrowed from me.

This is the woman who taught me to use a computer.

No matter how much you love your dog, you cannot refer to it as a *who.* It's *the hair of the dog that bit me,* not *the hair of the dog who bit me.*

THE GRAMMAR POLICE APPROACH

Any self-respecting Grammar Police officer can tell you that *which* introduces a clause that is *not* essential to the meaning of the sentence (a *nonrestrictive* clause). *That* introduces a clause that *is* essential to the meaning of the sentence (a *restrictive* clause). *Restrictive* sounds like a description of a whalebone corset. Ouch! And *nonrestrictive* seems almost irresponsible. Another problem with the Grammar Police terminology is that nagging questions keep arising: Who is restricting what? Why are they restricting it? And what business is it of theirs, anyway? Fortunately, answers are at hand.

Restrictive means that it restricts the *meaning of the sentence*. A restrictive clause is one that you must include in order for the sentence to convey your meaning. Notice in the above sentence that if you removed *that you must include,* you would end up with the sentence *a restrictive clause is one.* This sentence clearly lacks guts, so we know that the *that* phrase *is* essential to the sentence.

In comparison, a clause that is *not* essential to the meaning of the sentence is a *nonrestrictive clause.* These clauses are introduced by the word *which.* For example, in the sentence

> By that time, the IRS, which had been after him for years, had finally caught up with him.

You could omit *which had been after him for years* and still end up with the core sentence *by that time the IRS had finally caught up with him.* Because what really matters is that they finally caught the scoundrel, no matter how long it took them.

Which approach should you adopt? If you want to be careful and proper, follow the Grammar Police. If you're writing informally, just do it.

I HOPE THIS MAKES IT CLEAR

"Is that clear?"

Do you recall a teacher—or perhaps a parent—towering over you and asking this question? As you nodded mutely, you may have asked yourself, "What is *that?* What am I supposed to be clear about?"

In general, *this* refers to something nearby or present. If two things have already been mentioned, *this* refers to the one *nearer* in place, time, or thought. In contrast, *that* indicates something pointed out or present, that has been *mentioned before*. If two or more things have already been mentioned, *that* refers to the one *more remote* in place, time, or thought.

This and *that* can also be used as adjectives or as pronouns. When used as adjectives, they restrict the meaning to only one possibility. Ironically, when used as pronouns, they are capable of implying vast panoramas of potential but ambiguous meaning.

This or *that* used as adjectives:

Not that one! I want this one.

This ice cream is fat-free; that one is sugar-free.

This or *that* used as pronouns:

That is exactly what I'm talking about!

What is all this?

This capacity to indicate either great specificity or total ambiguity is just one of the pitfalls of using *this* and *that*.

ANOTHER HAZARD OF THIS AND THAT

The singular adjective forms of *this* and *that* are sometimes confused with their plural cousins, *these* and *those*. Here is this mistake in action:

This kind of envelopes don't seal well.

Which should be:

This kind of envelope *doesn't* seal well.

or

These kinds of envelopes *don't* seal well.

Although you will not die from mixing up *this* and *that*, it does make you sound ignorant, which isn't good.

Mixing up the singular and plural forms of *this* and *that* is a faux pas. However, abusing these words when they are pronouns can be fatal to your meaning. For example:

High interest rates, inflated prices, and low turnover have unsettled the housing market for several years; this means that homes must now be priced conservatively.

What means that homes must be priced conservatively? The rates? The prices? The turnover rate? If that example didn't convince you, try this:

Until now, your membership warehouse has stressed cost savings through quantity bulk sales and quick inventory turnover in a no-frills environment. This should change as the competition in the marketplace increases.

Put yourself in your reader's place. Assume that your reader is asking himself, "This *what*? What will change? The bulk sales? The quick turnover? The no-frills environment?"

Resist the temptation to use *this* and *that* as magic wands. You cannot wave them across your reader's eyes and be confident that he will know what you mean. Clarify *this* and *that*, and then you will never have to hear the question, "This what?"

I hope this makes it clear.

KISS AND MAKE-UP . . . OR KISS AND MAKE UP?

Many common phrases can indicate both actions and things. For example, you may need someone to help you *set up* your new stereo *set-up*. A person might *come back* to an expensive restaurant after experiencing a financial *come-back*.

The context of the sentence usually makes it clear to your reader whether you are referring to a verb (*to set up, to come back*, etc.) or a noun (*a set-up, a come-back*, etc.). However, the format of the sentence should also clarify your meaning.

If you want your reader to bundle two words together and see them as a noun, use a *hyphen* to show which words belong together. Here are a few more examples:

VERB–ADVERB COMBINATION	NOUN
The adverb answers the question: *How was the action done?*	The noun answers the question: *What is it?*
Make up	Make-up
"I will make up my mind soon."	"Her make-up looked awful."
Set up	Set-up
"I set it up that way."	"What a great set-up!"
Drive in	Drive-in
"Drive in there and you'll see the parking-lot attendant."	"We went to a drive-in movie."

Get up	Get-up
"Get up now or we'll be late."	"Are you going out in that get-up?"
Pay off	Pay-off
"How long will it take you to pay off that loan?"	"He worked very hard, but he's finally seeing the pay-off."
Take out	Take-out
"Please take out the garbage."	"Take-out food is convenient, but it does create a lot of garbage."

TENSE ABOUT TENSES?

Time is a great teacher, but unfortunately it kills all its pupils.
    —Hector Berlioz

It's probably just an accident that the word used to describe various expressions of time—*tense*—is the same one that is used to describe an extreme degree of emotional discomfort, right? Fortunately, after you read the next few pages, you need never be tense about tenses again.

First, let's consider what tenses do. They enable us to do something in language that we are unable to do in reality: move around in time. Imagine a language that could only use the present tense. You could not plan for tomorrow because you would have no word to describe it. You could not learn from the past because you would have no way to record it. You would be stuck in the eternal present. And while the idea of staying *in the now* has a certain charm from a philosophical standpoint, it's not a very effective way of building a society. Hence, tenses.

PERFECTION ITSELF

There are six basic tenses in English:

Simple past	Past perfect
Simple present	Present perfect
Simple future	Future perfect

The tense of a verb shows the time of an action—present, past, or future. The *present tense* shows that an action takes place now.

He fills the cup and drinks.

The *past tense* shows that an action took place at some previous time.

He filled the cup and drank.

The *future tense* shows that an action will take place in time to come.

He will fill the cup and he will drink.

The term *perfect tense* comes from the original Latin meaning of the word *perfect*. Literally, the word means *completely finished*. Those Romans were such perfectionists—they assumed that if something was finished, it must be flawless. Artists who tried to pass off flawed productions as *perfect* were probably thrown to the lions. Thus, the word *perfect* has come to mean *flawless*. However, in grammatical terms, all *perfect* means is *finished*. Isn't that a relief?

Perfect tenses show that an action is completed or *perfected* at the present, at some past time, or at some future time. They are formed by adding helping verbs such as *is, have, has* or *had,* or *shall have (will have)* to the past participle.

Present perfect tense shows that an action is complete at present. The action indicated began in the past and extends to the present or bears on the present.

> I have tried to explain this to him several times.

(My explanation began in the past and continues into the present.)

If two events occurred in the present, but one began before the present moment and one is occurring in the present moment, then use the present perfect and the simple present.

> I have been allergic to cats all my life, but now my symptoms are much worse.

Past perfect tense shows that an action was completed before another action in the past or completed before a definite time in the past:

> I had explained it to him many times before.

(My explanation was completed in the past—but did he listen?)

If two events occurred in the past, the one that happened earlier gets the *had been* tense, and the other one gets the simple past tense:

> I had told him several times not to use my car, but he used it anyway.

(I told him *before* he used it.)

The *future perfect tense* shows that an action will be completed before another action in the future or before a given time in the future. The future perfect tense is seldom used.

After my next explanation, I will have explained it to him twenty times.

In short, using tenses need not be tough. What's tough is effectively using the time they describe. As Benjamin Franklin said, "You may delay, but time will not."

DON'T GET LOST IN TIME

Who controls the past controls the future. Who controls the present controls the past.
          —George Orwell

When you want to describe events that happened at different times, be sure to follow a clear and logical time order in your descriptions. Many principles dictate how tenses can be combined in which ways, but the basic rule is that *it has to make sense.*

Stay in the same tense throughout the sentence or paragraph unless you have a clear and rational reason to do otherwise. If you begin your sentence in the present tense, complete it in the present tense unless you have sound logical reasons for changing the tense. If you begin in the past, end in the past. Guess what you should do if you begin in the future. Right.

Correct:

He believed that he was God. or He believes that he is God.

Incorrect:

He believed that he is God.

Correct:

He believes that his child is a genius.

He believes that his child will be a genius.

He believes that all children are potential geniuses.

Incorrect:

He believed that his child is a genius.

He will believe that his child was a genius.

Correct:

Loose lips sink ships.

God provides.

(These are correct because eternal truths can always be expressed in the present tense.)

Sequencing events accurately might seem confusing, but you can simplify the process. *Speak the sentence slowly out loud, and you will find that you can usually get it straight.* If you still don't feel it's clear, then draw a time line and list the events in sequence. And if you still can't follow the sequence, *recast the whole sentence.* Remember that it's no crime to use several sentences to describe a sequence of events. If you cannot easily figure out the correct time sequence, you should probably rework the sentence anyway. In fact, creating several sentences is usually a good solution to the problem of time confusion within one sentence. If you can't follow the sequence of events in the sentence, your reader probably won't be able to either.

Part 8.

Mark My Punctuation!

Punctuation sets the rhythm and pace of your writing. It can also affect your meaning. Did you hear about the prisoner whose life was spared because of a punctuation error? The prisoner stood on the gallows with the noose around his neck, praying that his request for a last-minute pardon would be granted. The governor telegraphed: "Pardon impossible. To be executed immediately." But the telegraph operator transcribed: "Pardon. Impossible to be executed immediately." The prisoner was released. Punctuation is powerful!

Before you punctuate, ask yourself:

- How would I *speak* this sentence out loud?
- What *function* will the punctuation serve here? Am I *ending* a sentence, *introducing* a portion of the sentence, *separating* parts of the sentence, or *enclosing* a parenthetical phrase?
- What *rules* of punctuation apply?

FUNCTIONAL AND DYSFUNCTIONAL PUNCTUATION

If you've read your sentence aloud and still aren't sure how to punctuate it, ask yourself what function you want the punctuation mark to serve. Punctuation plays four basic roles:

1. To end a statement (use period, question mark, or exclamation point):

   Little work was done.

   Are you leaving now?

   This is outrageous!

2. To introduce (use comma, dash, or colon):

   Only one thing is needed: money.

   Whatever is, is for the good.

   The course is obvious—fire him.

3. To separate parts of a sentence or word (use a comma, semicolon, dash, hyphen, or apostrophe. A semicolon functions as a kind of weakened period. Use it to connect two independent clauses that are logically related):

   Their train was late; they'll be late.

   If you had any kindness at all, you would bring me something to eat.

   Some people work better in the morning; others work best at night.

   Commas, periods, semicolons, and colons—these are all marks of punctuation.

4. To enclose parts of a sentence or a whole sentence (use commas, dashes, quotation marks, single quotation marks, parentheses, or brackets. Enclosure marks are used in pairs, except when the capital letter at the beginning of a sentence takes the place of the first or when a terminating mark at the end takes the place of the second):

You, my dear friend, are my last resort.

John said, "Please take a number."

The Internal Revenue Service (IRS) is not known for its informality.

You are not—and everyone knows this—a man of discretion.

A few other punctuation points follow their own rules. Colons, semicolons, dashes, hyphens, and apostrophes will be explained in the next few pages. Reading aloud and checking for function will answer most of your punctuation questions.

LISTEN FOR PUNCTUATION AS YOU READ YOUR WORK ALOUD

You can usually resolve your doubts about punctuation by reading the questionable sentence aloud. A full stop indicates a period. A pause generally indicates a comma. A rising, questioning intonation usually indicates a question mark. When you stop speaking abruptly but make it clear that some related statement is immediately to follow, you will probably be using a colon.

Reading aloud enables your ears to help you correct mistakes that you have literally overlooked. Your eyes may fool you into inserting periods and commas where they do not belong, but your ears will stop you from inserting too much punctuation.

USE COMMAS CAREFULLY

Commas are frequent troublemakers in business writing: People use too few, or too many, or they use them where they should have used a period or semicolon. The function of a comma is to introduce or separate parts of a sentence.

To introduce: *In short, proper punctuation is vital to clear writing.*

To separate: *Learning to write well, a task which people often avoid, is a necessity for business success.*

Read your work aloud and most of your comma problems will be solved. As you read, insert a comma where your voice pauses. You may wish to practice this skill by reading a variety of documents aloud and noting where the commas are placed.

Despite its value in helping you parse information, a comma cannot end a sentence. Do not rely on the comma to do the job of a period! Using a comma instead of a period is called a *comma splice*. For example, this sentence is incorrect:

> The off-site training seminar was very informative, we
> gained both technical and team-building skills.

It should in fact be two sentences:

> The off-site training seminar was very informative. We
> gained both technical and team-building skills.

The general trend in business writing today is toward using fewer commas. This is fine—as long as you remember to check the naturalness, clarity, correctness, and flow of your work by reading it aloud.

USING COMMAS: THE SERIES

The question of whether to put a comma before the last item in a series ranks high among the many debates that rage among business writers. The answer to this question is an unequivocal "It depends."

- Using a comma between the next-to-last and the last item on a list is **optional.** If you are making a list of things or places, it is not necessary to put a comma between the last item on the list and the word *and*.

Please buy pens, pencils, blank diskettes, paper clips and staples.

- If the sentence flows better with a comma at the end of the series, then it is okay to use it.
- If you are listing names in a professional partnership such as a law firm, then you should insert a comma between the next-to-last name and the final name.

They've retained the law firm of Martin, Christianson, Moskowitz, and O'Brian.

APOSTROPHE APOSTASY

Notice at a sports club:

Please wear shoe's in the pool area.

Welcome sign at a museum:

Visitor's are kindly requested to sign the register.

Sign at a photocopy shop:

Ask the cashier for this weeks list.

*The apostrophe is used mainly in hand-lettered small business signs
to alert the reader than an "S" is coming up at the end of a word, as
in: WE DO NOT EXCEPT PERSONAL CHECK'S, or: NOT
RESPONSIBLE FOR ANY ITEM'S. Another important grammar
concept to bear in mind when creating hand-lettered small-business
signs is that you should put quotation marks around random words
for decoration, as in "TRY" OUR HOT DOG'S, or even TRY "OUR"
HOT DOG'S.*

   —Dave Barry, "Tips for Writer's"

Grammatical errors undermine your credibility, especially
when they appear in business documents. One such error
that has crept stealthily into print in recent years is one that
everyone supposedly learned in the third grade: when and
how to use the apostrophe-s combination.

There is no grammatical basis for using an apostrophe-s
ending to signify a plural. You can write one cat, two cats.
One shoe, two shoes. Or if you want to get fancy, one company, two companies. But *never* write *shoe's* if what you mean
is that there are *two shoes*.

Why is there this compulsion to apostrophize? Do people
vaguely recall that an apostrophe sometimes goes before the
s—so they pop them into words at random and hope that now
and then they get it right? These grammar gaffes make me
grumpy.

Okay, so when *do* you use an apostrophe?

- *To indicate that a letter or letters have been omitted.* For
  example, instead of *let us see,* you could write, *let's see.*
  Or—watch out here, this gets tricky—instead of *it is,*
  you could write *it's.*

- *To show possession.* Instead of having to write, *This shoe belongs to John*, we can write *John's shoe.* Instead of saying, *Hey—I think that is the car that belongs to John.* you can say, *Hey—I think that's John's car.* What a deal!
- *To show* both *a plural and possession.* If you have one cat, and the cat has a bowl, then you could write, *The cat's bowl is in the kitchen.*

But suppose that your cat got out one night and visited some tomcat that didn't even remember her name in the morning—and that now you have six cats. First, you must buy a much bigger bowl. Then you could write, *The cats' bowl is in the kitchen.* Many cats possess the bowl. We convey this by putting an s-apostrophe at the end of the word.

SMITHS, SMITH'S, OR SMITHS'

A few years ago a woman called my office; she seemed to be in great distress. "I hope that you can help me," she said, "I need a piece of information right now." I said I would try to answer her question. She asked, "If a word ends in s, how do you write it in possessive form?" I explained that contemporary usage differs from what she might have been taught in school. At one time, we put an apostrophe after the final s in words that ended in s. For example, we would write

the countess' tiara

the Simmons' guest

the Grand Tetons' ecology

Ah, those were the good old days. However, for reasons known only to the gods of grammar, the current rule is this:

Words that end in s become possessive when you add the 's regardless of whether the word ends in s. The only exceptions to this rule are major historical figures, such as Moses, Jesus, Confucius, and Xerxes. So we might write:

> *According to Moses' law, the Simmons's guest is culpable for having stolen the countess's tiara. Jesus' teachings might recommend that the countess should turn the other cheek, but of course Xerxes' law would have been to chop off the fellow's head.*

"Thank God!" said the woman gratefully.

"I hope you don't mind my asking," I said, "but why was it so important for you to know this?" She said, "All my life I've been asking my great-uncle for answers to any grammar questions. In fact, our entire family calls him for grammar advice. Last week, I asked him about the possessive form, and he told me about Jesus and Confucius and Xerxes, and I thought he must have finally been going senile. His kids were talking about putting him in a nursing home. I am so relieved to know that he was right."

She said good-bye, and I returned to my work with the satisfaction of knowing that perhaps I'd saved a fellow grammar buff from involuntary institutionalization.

THE SECRET OF THE SEMICOLON

Many people suffer from secret feelings of stupidity because they don't know how to use the semicolon. They imagine that everyone else knows what to do with this sophisticated mark of punctuation—and that they must have been absent or dreaming on the one day of school when the teacher explained it. Since they assume that everyone else knows the secret of the semicolon, they are usually too embarrassed to admit their own ignorance. The truth is that very few people know how to use the semicolon correctly, and the semicolon is incredibly easy to use.

SEMICOLONS: THE WHOLE TRUTH

A *semicolon* has three major functions:

1. It connects two independent clauses that are logically related and that are not joined by a conjunction.

Give without remembering; take without forgetting.

2. It separates items on a list, especially when the items on the list contain commas.

We visited the following cities: Paris, France; London, England; Rome, Italy; and Geneva, Switzerland.

3. It separates independent clauses if there are commas within the clauses.

We own a sailboat, a catamaran, and a motor boat; still, our favorite maritime activity is lolling around on deck.

HOW TO TELL IF YOU HAVE USED THE SEMICOLON CORRECTLY IN A SENTENCE

When you use the semicolon within a sentence, you should be able to replace the semicolon with a period. The words on the left and the right sides of the semicolon must be able to stand alone meaningfully without any further revision.

In short, the semicolon:

- Functions like a conjunction
- Separates two independent clauses
- Separates items on a list, especially when the list was introduced by a colon.

Think of it as a weakened period—as you can see from its structure, the semicolon is partly a period and partly a comma. Never let yourself be intimidated by a semicolon. It is just a punctuation mark. Period.

AND YOU CAN QUOTE ME—BUT HOW?

Writers oten get "creative" in their use of quotation marks, leading to many quotation mark miscues. The basic function of quotation marks is to enclose direct quotes. Stick to this usage and you won't go wrong. (Remember that a direct quote is exactly what the person said, word for word—not pretty much what they said, or what you think they meant.)

When the quotation is part of a sentence, the quotation marks go *outside* the final punctuation mark of the sentence you are quoting. So it's "So long, it's been good to know you." This principle is easy to remember when you consider that the stop at the end of the sentence is actually part of what that person said. The punctuation mark that signals the end of the sentence is also part of the quote and thus belongs within the quotation marks. Here are some of the other uses of quotation marks:

Use quotation marks the first time you use a new term:

> A "veggie burger" is like a hamburger. The main difference is
> that the veggie burger is made of chopped vegetables
> instead of chopped beef.

(Note that *veggie burger* is only placed within quotation marks the first time it is used.)

Use quotation marks to enclose text following terms such as:

entitled

> The musical entitled "Hair" is not about a beauty shop.

the word

> The word "cyberwonk" should not be used in polite company.

marked

> The bottle marked "Drink me" made Alice small.

designated

> Do not park in spaces that are designated "reserved."

referred to as

> The kid referred to as "the House" weighed 250 pounds.

If you are quoting more than one paragraph from a text, signal your reader that you are inserting a long quotation by indenting and single-spacing the quotation.

When quoting more than two lines, indent and single space the whole quotation. This is called a *block quote*.

When quoting several paragraphs, put quotation marks *before the first word of each paragraph* in the quotation. Do not put quotation marks at the end of a paragraph if the following paragraph is part of the same quote. By putting quotation marks at the beginning of each quoted paragraph, you tell your reader that this paragraph is a continuation of the quote. When you want to signal that the whole quotation is finished, place quotation marks at the end of the last paragraph of the quote.

Use quotation marks to enclose titles of articles, poems, stories, speeches, and parts of whole printed works. (Titles of periodicals, books, plays, operas, motion pictures, radio and television series, and other complete works are italicized.)

John J. Donne wrote an article called "Use of the Sonnet Form in Contemporary Music" in a recent issue of Poetry Today.

For an exhaustive (sometimes exhausting) review of every rule related to quotation marks and punctuation, check the latest edition of the *Chicago Manual of Style*.

MINIMIZE "CUTE" QUOTATION MARKS

If you want to use quotation marks as a cute way to express a feeling, draw as many funny pictures as you want, but do not put quotation marks around words to indicate a trendy usage. Once you stray into the realms of "cutesy," "hip," or "ironic" quotation marks, you're asking for "trouble."

QUOTATION MARK NO-NO'S

Don't use quotation marks to set off an indirect quote. An indirect quote implies that the writer has paraphrased the contents of the original quote. For example, if I say that

Strunk and White abhorred extremely long sentences, that would be an indirect quote.

Don't use quotation marks to help people realize that what you've written is meant to be taken with a grain of salt. Don't even use them to demonstrate that you know you're using a word that is too informal for the context in which you are writing. If the word is wrong for the context, perhaps you ought not use it. Just remember, "Quotation marks are for quotations."

SEX AND THE SINGLE QUOTATION MARK

See? I already got your attention with "sex." Single quotation marks often lament that they are not welcomed into polite conversation as often as are quotation marks in pairs. Nevertheless, single quotes serve an important function: They enable writers to enclose quotations within quotations. If you happen to be quoting two individuals within the same passage, the single quotation mark enables you to tell one speaker from another. For example,

> Mr. Jones, the storeowner, arrived one morning and found that his safe had been stolen from the back of the store. He asked the night manager what had happened. The manager replied, "Sally was supposed to lock up last night. But just before I left, I heard Sally whispering, 'Get that thing off my foot. It's heavy.'"

Note that at the end of the quote-within-a-quote, you have a single quotation mark next to a double quotation mark. This looks odd, but it is correct.

RELATIONSHIP SECRETS OF QUOTATION MARKS

Like the rest of us, quotation marks must learn to live with their neighbors. Quotations within sentences require quotation marks, but the other parts of the sentence have needs, too. Here's how you can make all your punctuation marks work together.

For a quotation within a sentence, do not capitalize the first word in the quotation:

> Many writing instructors tell you to "just say no" to excessive quotation marks.

For a quotation that begins within the sentence and continues to the end of the sentence, introduce the quotation with a comma and place the quotation marks outside the quote:

> Eve said, "Go ahead and eat it. It's organic."

Sometimes quotations meet exclamation points or question marks. Remember that the strong feeling conveyed by ! or the question implied by ? is part of the quotation itself. Since these punctuation marks convey the tone of the message, they belong inside the quotation marks.

> "Are you nuts?" shouted Adam. "Don't you know that stuff has been genetically engineered?"

For a quotation that begins and ends within the sentence, introduce the quotation with a comma and end it with a comma. Even if the quotation ends with a period, change the period into a comma when inserting the quotation into the middle of a sentence. As always, the quotation marks belong outside the quotation's punctuation marks.

> *"I disapprove of what you say," wrote the French philosopher Voltaire, "but I will defend to the death your right to say it."*

When a quotation shares a sentence with a semicolon or colon, place the quotation marks before the semicolon or colon:

> *It seemed that they had found the proverbial "smoking gun"; this discovery put the tobacco industry in deep trouble with gun manufacturers.*

> *I told my boss I wanted a raise and he had only one thing to say: "So what?"*

SCOPING OUT THE COLON

The colon helps you orchestrate the speed at which your reader reads. Most people fly straight through a sentence that has no internal punctuation marks—just as you flew through the last sentence you read. A comma within the sentence forces the reader to pause, even briefly, before he continues his headlong run. The colon creates a stop within the sentence or within the thought. Thus, it increases the dramatic impact of the information that follows it. For example,

> *There's only one thing this company needs: money.*

This sentence puts a strong emphasis on *money*. If you want to put less emphasis on the pecuniary, you could write the same idea as

The only thing this company needs is money.

The difference is subtle but real. Both sentences are grammatically correct, but their nuances are different.

HYPHENS ARE WORD GLUE

Hyphens either glue several words together or show where words should be broken apart. When you combine several nouns or adjectives to make them into one noun or adjective, use the hyphen to show the reader which words belong together. For example, *set up* could be a verb-adverb combination while *set-up* is unquestionably a noun. *Take out* is also a verb-adverb combination, but *take-out* is a kind of cuisine.

He was all set up to take me out for take-out. He wanted to eat at his place so that he could show me his new stereo set-up.

If you're not sure whether to hyphenate a word combination, ask yourself whether the reader could misunderstand the phrase on first reading. If so, then hyphenate. In short, use hyphens to:

- Create new words by combining two or more other words.
man-made materials

day-old bread

safe-haven rules

case-by-case basis

die-hard

contractor-requested recalculations

- Prevent ambiguity.

Recreation is a leisure activity. Re-creation is the process of making something over again.

- Prevent awkward spelling. Imagine this without hyphens:

My exwife bought a tshirt for my exboss.

- Show where to break a word at the end of a line of text.

Rules about hyphen usage change more rapidly than rules about other aspects of grammar. Words that require hyphens today might not require them a few years from now. "Basketball" originated as a two-word phrase, "basket ball." As the game became more established it was known as "basket-ball." After a while, sports writers got tired of adding that hyphen when everyone knew that they were talking about the game of basketball, so they dispensed with the hyphen. The same process is already happening with words like e-mail and cyber-space. When e-mail was introduced it was always hyphenated. However, most people now write "email."

Watch established publications like the *Wall Street Journal* or the *New York Times* for clues to contemporary usage.

DON'T DASH BY

Dash dash dash has lost a lot of meaning since the days of Morse code. Today, the dash is like the superficial peck on the cheek in Hollywood: It implies relationship without commitment. In casual writing, dashes may stand in for parentheses or commas as a way of inserting a piece of new information or a pause into a sentence. They lend a breezy air to your messages—sometimes a little too breezy. Smattering your work with handfuls of dashes can undermine your credibility because it gives the impression that you didn't stop to think about what you were writing—you just—kind of—dashed across the page. These are the hazards in using dashes:

- Dashes are very informal, so don't use them in formal business correspondence or with readers who are sticklers for tradition.
- Dashes make it easy for you to gloss over gaps in organization and logic. Shame on you if you thought this was a benefit! It is a drawback. Your reader will not dash so nimbly over the logical gaps between your thoughts.

Nowadays, the most common use of dashes seems to be this: They create an illusion of punctuation in sentences that are actually not well structured. The writer is careening around some grammatical corner and suddenly realizes that he's introduced an entirely new idea, or made a tangential comment, or that he isn't sure whether to end the sentence or not. So he throws in a string of dashes, and the sentence seems to hang together. Not. Unless you are writing an extremely informal note to a close friend, don't punctuate with dashes.

PARENTHETICALLY SPEAKING

Parentheses have two major functions: They help connect long names and terms to shorter acronyms and nicknames, and they enable you to interject peripheral information into a sentence or paragraph.

Parentheses are handy when you are introducing an acronym, abbreviation, or nickname.

> The Federal Bureau of Investigation (FBI) has branches all over the United States of America (USA).

> General Aerodynamic Internet (GAI) has hired Wise and Brilliant Consultants (the consultant) to perform a very expensive study of paper-clip usage among administrative personnel (study).

Parentheses also allow you to insert peripheral comments or ideas into a sentence or paragraph. This is a mixed blessing. Often the witticism that ends up in parentheses is merely a synaptic hiccup posing as an idea. Think carefully about whether your parenthetical comment deserves to be included in your sentence at all. If it's really significant, it probably should not be in parentheses. If it's really irrelevant, it probably should not be in the document. When you do insert a parenthetical phrase, limit it to a few words. Here's another reason to limit the length of text within parentheses. Read the following sentence:

> Now is the time for all good men (at least, the men who think they're good and want to be considered good by the people who really matter) to come to the aid of their country.

After you finished reading the contents of the parentheses, were you able to pick up the second half of the sentence and integrate it instantly into the first? Or did you have to start reading the sentence again? Few readers have the concentration or the commitment to read a long parenthetical phrase without forgetting the first part of the sentence. Your parenthetical material must be brief enough that the reader can absorb it without having to reread the sentence. If not, you put the reader in the frustrating position of having to read the first half of the sentence and hold it in mind as he reads the parenthetical phrase. He must then hold the parenthetical phrase in mind as he reads the second half of the sentence, integrates the first and second halves of the sentence, and then further integrates the contents of the parentheses into the sentence as he has finally understood it. Not likely.

PUNCTUATION ABUSE

Another sport that wastes unlimited time is comma hunting. Once start a comma hunt and the whole pack will be off, full cry, especially if they have had a literary training. . . . But comma-hunting is so exciting as to be a little dangerous. When attention is entirely concentrated on punctuation, there is some fear that the conduct of business may suffer, and a proposal get through without being properly obstructed on its demerits. It is therefore wise, when a kill has been made, to move at once for adjournment.
    —*Francis M. Cornford*

If you have tried to punctuate your sentence in a variety of ways and it still doesn't seem right, ask yourself if punctuation is really the problem. Often, what seems like a punctuation error is really a writing problem. If you know that something is wrong, and you think that you could fix it if you just knew where to put the comma or semicolon, think again. Read the sentence aloud and see if perhaps the whole thing needs to be rewritten. Many punctuation questions disappear when your sentence structure is strong.

Part 9.

RE-VISION MEANS SEEING AGAIN

Am returning this otherwise good typing paper to you because some-one has printed gibberish all over it and put your name at the top.
    —English professor

Many people believe that if only they were smart enough, talented enough, or lucky enough, they would be able to write a perfect first draft. This fantasy is about as realistic as imagining that if only they could flap their arms like a bird does, they could fly. Even the greatest writers revise their work dozens of times. Original manuscripts from Shakespeare, Tolstoy, and other literary geniuses show that they ruthlessly and repeatedly revised their work. If they did it, we can too. As the adage says, "Writing is rewriting what has already been rewritten."

This section of *Get to the Point* tells you when and how to revise your work. Just as important, it tells you when to stop revising. As you revise, you compare your original vision for this document with what you have actually written. No matter how good, smart, or well intentioned you are, there will be gaps between your initial vision and your first draft. Sometimes they'll be big gaps. Sometimes they will be impassable chasms. Editing is the process of bridging the gaps if you can or figuring out an entirely different route if you must.

Revising a document is like sanding a piece of furniture. You sand the wood for a while and then check to see if it is smooth yet. You sense a few bumps or rough edges, so you sand it some more. You check it again and sand it again, over and over until the wood looks and feels right. Similarly, you revise your document over and over until the whole thing flows smoothly. If you have any doubts, then keep revising. You may need to rearrange your points, streamline your sentence structure, or recast a few sentences in the active voice. If there are too many words on the page, cut the ones that don't carry their weight. As Antoine de St. Exupéry, author of *The Little Prince* and other classics, said, "Perfection is achieved, not when there is nothing left to add, but when there is nothing left to take away."

*Whenever you feel an impulse to perpetrate a piece of exceptionally fine writing, obey it—wholeheartedly—and delete it before sending your manuscripts to press. **Murder your darlings.***
—Sir Arthur Quiller-Couch

GENERAL PRINCIPLES OF EDITING

1. Do not edit as you write.

Begin editing only after you have finished your first draft.

2. After you finish writing, put the work aside before you begin to revise.

Let it rest overnight if you can. If that's impossible, at least take a break or a walk, or have a snack before you begin to edit.

3. Edit in stages.

Scan the structure and organization first. After correcting errors in planning and large-scale construction, read the document again for the next "pass" at editing. Revise sentence structure and refine word choice after you know the basic structure works.

I try to leave out the parts that people skip.
        —Elmore Leonard

DON'T EDIT AS YOU WRITE

Writing and editing are distinct processes: Don't muddle them together. Writing requires you to let the words flow as they come to you. Editing requires you to stop and critically assess each word. It is hard to stay in the creative flow when you are stopping after every word to criticize what you've just written.

If you try to write your first draft and edit it at the same time, you're likely to lose your concentration and get caught up in details instead of delivering your message. When you second-guess yourself before you get your whole idea on paper, you're likely to end up with a draft that looks like this:

~~Dear Mr. Johnson,~~ Dear Fred,

~~Thank you for your interest in~~ thank you for asking about ~~here is the information you~~ thank you for requesting

~~thank you for asking for~~ information about ~~our company~~ our ~~firm our~~ product line.

By the time you finish the first paragraph, you are likely to be frustrated, exasperated, out of time, and unable to remember what you originally intended to say.

Here are several ways to overcome the urge to change your writing before you have written it:

- If you are not sure whether a particular word or phrase is right, put brackets around it. [The bracketed text will look like this.] After you finish the draft, edit the bracketed words first.
- If you are in the middle of writing and you realize that you don't have a piece of information that you need, do not stop writing to go and look it up. Simply put in a set of brackets to remind yourself of the missing data. Look it up later and plug it in.
- Write straight through your first draft. Drafting is much easier when you write straight through, and editing is much easier when you have a finished draft to work from.

PUT IT ASIDE

Editing requires coolness, objectivity, and ruthlessness. Editing often requires you to "murder your darlings."

The best way to develop objectivity about your work is to let some time pass after you write it. Ideally, you should not edit your work on the same day that you write it. Come back to the document after a good night's sleep. You will see it more clearly.

The Brilliant Business Letter:
A Modern Fable

Once upon a time, there was a business owner who had to write a very important letter to her key client. She dashed off the letter in a frenzy of inspiration, printed it, signed it, and dropped it in the mailbox as she left the office. On the way home, she chuckled to herself over some of the clever lines she had included in the letter. She pictured her client calling her and saying that he'd decided to buy twice as much of her product as he had previously intended.

The next morning, she came into office and picked up the copy of the letter that she had kept for her files. Her face suddenly drained of color. She realized that she had referred to his family, forgetting that his wife and children had recently left him. She had referred to a conversation they'd had at a social event—and she now remembered that the client had not been invited to that event; she'd "remembered" a conversation that had not actually happened. She saw several spelling errors. She realized that her "clever" remarks were actually foolish and that they would probably offend her client. She thought of pillaging the mailbox in which she'd placed the letter the night before but remembered that she had been careful to choose a spot that had a late-night mail pickup. She thought of trying to bribe his secretary to return the letter to her without opening it. Finally, she steeled herself to wait for her client's angry call. The moral of the story is: **Never mail anything important on the day you write it.** (Note: This moral also applies to e-mail; think twice before you hit the "send" button. For more on effective e-mail, see pages 221–23.)

STAGES OF EDITING

The revision process mirrors the writing process. You created your document first by establishing your purpose, then by organizing your information into an appropriate structure, and then by drafting strong sentences and choosing the right words. You will revise by retracing your steps through each of these stages of production. The key difference is that when you write, you see through your own eyes; when you revise, you try to see the document through your reader's eyes. Picture your reader reading it, and ask yourself, "Is this person finding it easy to pay attention? Is my meaning clear? Have I achieved my purpose?" These are the major stages of editing:

1. Fix the structure.
2. Strengthen your sentences.
3. Review your word choice.
4. Proofread for spelling and punctuation.
5. Be sure that the format is clean and consistent.
6. When you're all done, send it out and don't think about it anymore.

Should you go through all these steps? Probably you should, even if you move through them very quickly. Skipping any one of them leaves you vulnerable to undermining your entire message and rendering the rest of your efforts futile.

STAGE ONE: FIX THE STRUCTURE FIRST

Edit your document's organization before you edit the writing. Remember that organizing and writing are separate processes. It is nearly impossible to write successfully if you try to write and organize simultaneously in one rough draft. It is just as unwise to edit simultaneously for organizational and writing errors.

Imagine that you have built a chair. After finishing your "rough draft" of the chair, the first thing you will check is to see whether it will serve the essential functions of a chair. Even the most avant-garde chair has a seat and some kind of legs. Next you will test whether the chair is solidly put together. There's no point having a nifty new chair if it falls over the first time someone sits on it. The parts need to be structured so that they fit together, and their connections to each other must be solid. Similarly, you need to check the strength of your document's basic structure before tweaking your word choice and sentence structure. It would be a shame to spend time fine-tuning verbiage and then end up deleting the entire sentence or paragraph as part of a larger restructuring.

STAGE ONE CHECKLIST:
PLANNING AND ORGANIZATION

1. Read it once through quickly.

Get an overview of the whole piece so that you can see its general strengths and weaknesses. Put check marks in the margin next to sentences that are likely to need a lot of work, but don't edit them until you move on to the next editing stage.

2. Read it again, focusing on the three P's.

❏ Is the purpose clear? If it is not clear, what information must you add or delete in order to fulfill your purpose?

❏ Have you highlighted the points that benefit the reader?

❏ Are you clear about your main point? Will your reader be clear about it?

3. Read it again, focusing on organization.

❏ Have your included the right ideas and the necessary information? Will these words, in this order, carry your thought into your reader's mind?

❏ Have you put your main point first? If not, why not?

❏ Is the organizational structure consistent throughout?

❏ Does each paragraph introduce a new topic?

When you feel that the structure of your document is sound, then proceed to the next level of editing.

STAGE TWO: STRENGTHEN YOUR SENTENCES

Make everything as simple as possible, but not simpler.
        —Albert Einstein

If you need to have surgery, you want the surgeon to remove only the tissue that is making you sick. You wouldn't want him saying, "As long as I'm in here, I might as well yank that pancreas." Similarly, when you perform surgery on your sentences, be sure you retain the vital words: the subject, the verb, and the connecting words that show how all the parts of the sentence are related.

In the process of editing their work, writers sometimes delete crucial portions of their sentences. They do this because they believe they are streamlining their work by taking a few words out. The problem is that they take the wrong words out, leaving their reader perplexed about the real meaning of the sentence. This is like a doctor operating to take out the tonsils and instead taking out the vocal cords. Writing malpractice! The secret to good writing is to leave the important words in and take the extra ones out. Search for the point at which you have the maximum meaning with the minimum words.

When in doubt, strike it out.
        —Mark Twain

STAGE TWO CHECKLIST:

SENTENCE STRUCTURE

☐ Do the subject and the verb agree—singular nouns linked to singular verbs and plural nouns linked to plural verbs?

☐ Is the pronoun reference clear?

☐ Is the "person" consistent (all *I*, all *you*, etc.)?

☐ Are there dangling modifiers or other unclear references?

☐ Is the sentence structure parallel, using similar structure for similar ideas?

☐ Is the sentence structure reasonably simple, with no more than two subordinate clauses? (As a rule, you should not have more than two phrases that start with *which, that, since,* or *because.*)

☐ Are you sure that this is not a run-on sentence? Be sure you haven't glued several sentence together with *and, or, but, whereas,* or other conjunctions.

☐ Is the sentence around 15 words long? If it's less than 15 words, that's great. If it's more than 17 words, see if you can omit any unnecessary words or split the sentence either at a relative pronoun or a conjunction.

If the sentence must exceed 17 words in order to convey this thought, then leave it alone. Reduce the length of surrounding sentences so that the average sentence length stays within 10 and 17 words.

STAGE THREE: REVIEW YOUR WORD CHOICE

The difference between the right word and the almost right word is the difference between lightning and the lightning bug.
    —Mark Twain

After you've checked the organization and sentence structure, read the document again, this time savoring the feeling and tone of each word. The range of connotation and nuance for every concept is immense. When considering word choice, take into account the different ways in which the reader comes to understand your language. Every word has one or more dictionary meanings as well as one or more connotations. You might think of the connotation as the emotional part of the word's meaning; it affects how the reader feels.

DICTIONARY MEANING

Are you sure that this word means what you think it does? If you are even a tiny bit uncertain of your word's meaning, take a moment and look it up in the dictionary. Don't embarrass yourself.

You might be tempted to use a word in an unusual context or as part of an offbeat image. Go right ahead if you must. However, if you use a word in a non-standard sense, realize that the reader may misunderstand you. Sometimes, alas, it is better to be understood than to be interesting.

WATCH OUT FOR UNINTENDED
DOUBLE MEANINGS

She ate the doughnuts with relish.

Fleeing leopards can be dangerous.

I saw her walking her dog, and then I saw her duck.

The only other food in the house was some iced tea, Kool-Aid, a few staples, and some frozen fish sticks that they would eat later for dinner. ("What's for dinner, Mom?" "Staples and Kool-Aid.")

Your word might have a straightforward meaning when you look it up in the dictionary and still be a ridiculous choice in the context of your sentence. As you revise, ask yourself not only whether it is the right word, but also whether the word retains your intended meaning in the sentence.

WHAT DOES IT MEAN TO YOUR READER?

Yup, it's that pesky reader again. Your word may mesh perfectly with the dictionary definition. It may look and sound great in your sentence. It may be one of your favorite words in the whole world. But if your reader won't understand it, you can't use it.

Consider *chartreuse*. I know that chartreuse is a color. But I must confess that I have never been sure exactly what color it is. I gather that it's the kind of color that interior designers use, but if you handed me a set of color swatches and asked me to select chartreuse, I could not do it. So if you were trying to describe a room to me, and if the sofa were the most perfect example of chartreuse ever to grace an interior design showroom, you still could not describe it to me (color ignoramus that I am) with the word *chartreuse*.

Similarly, you cannot describe a property's shape as *trapezoidal* if your reader might think that a trapezoid is something that circus performers swing on. You cannot describe a wine as having a *fine bouquet* and *long legs* if your reader thinks that wine comes in only three varieties: red, white, and bubbly.

When writing to clients and colleagues, use words in their standard meaning. Make sure that your words cannot be misunderstood or take on a different meaning in the context of your sentence. And narrow your vocabulary if that's what you must do to reach your reader. Remember: Readers rule!

STAGE THREE CHECKLIST: WORD CHOICE

1. Dictionary Meaning

❑ Do you understand the dictionary meaning of this word?

❑ Will your reader understand the basic meaning of this word?

2. Emotional Meaning (Connotation)

❑ What feeling do you want this word to convey?

❑ What other nuance (if any) do you hope to communicate?

❑ Given your knowledge of your reader, is it likely that this word will convey the desired feeling?

❑ If not, what comparable word would have the connotation you seek?

3. Contextual Meaning

❑ Does this word mean what you intend it to mean *in this sentence?*

   ❑ If a person were quickly scanning, could the context lead her to think that a word means something different than you intended?

   ❑ Will this word mean what you want it to mean *in this document?*

   ❑ Given the *social and cultural milieu* of your reader, will the word retain your desired meaning?

   Some words have specialized meanings within particular social or professional groups. Different nationalities use the same words to indicate very different meanings. Be careful!

STAGE FOUR: PROOFREAD CAREFULLY

Spelling a word wrong is like showing up for a meeting with a blob of ketchup on your shirt. Spelling, punctuation, quotation marks, consistency of format, page numbering, and margins are all important parts of your presentation. Errors in these areas plant doubts in the reader's mind about your competence. Do not rely on software programs to do all your proofreading. After you run spell-check, check your work yourself!

THE TURKEY PROPOSAL FOR THE PUBIC SECTOR: BEWARE OF THE SPELL-CHECK TYPO

Only you can save yourself from using sound-alikes that have nothing to do with your meaning. Your spell-checker will not rescue you from mistakes like these:

weather	*instead of*	*whether*
later		*latter*
base		*based*
decrease		*decreased*
four		*for*
form		*from*
too		*to*
singed		*signed*
turkey		*turnkey*

Begin proofreading *at the end* of the document and work your way to the beginning. By reading backward, you minimize the risk that you will "see" a word as correct when in reality it contains a typographical error.

Here's a good way to check your spelling: Cut a slit in your business card about the size of a word. Turn the card over and work through the document from back to front, word by word.

PERILS OF THE GRAMMAR CHECKER

Grammar-checking software gives me hope for the human race because it demonstrates that there is no substitute for human judgment. As cleverly designed as it may be, grammar-checking software cannot tell the difference between *their, there,* and *they're* in context. All it can do is point out that these words are frequently misused. Grammar-checking software cannot discern when a writer has used the passive voice appropriately. All it can do is point out that the sentence is in the passive voice.

In short, software has neither judgment nor any sense of nuance or context. It does not know why you are writing or to whom you are writing. All it can do is highlight deviations from standard usage and flag common grammar errors. This is a valuable service, and I recommend that you use grammar checkers for what they're worth. Just don't assume that the software program's opinion is always the one you should follow.

Remember to use your judgment wisely when you use this software. I taught a seminar for a roomful of financial analysts a few years ago. During our discussion on using the grammar-checking software, one woman raised her hand and said, "I get that message all the time: 'Sentence is in the passive voice.' But I don't know what to do about it!" Before I could answer, another participant's hand shot up. "I can tell you how to solve that problem," she cried. "There's a little square labeled 'Don't show me this again' in the bottom of the grammar checker's pop-up box. Just put an *x* there and you'll never get that message again."

The grammar checker points out some technical writing problems, but it does not always suggest a good way to solve them. Complex or abstract sentences are out of the range of grammar software; they need to be dealt with in hand-to-hand combat. That's part of the joy of being human.

My final piece of advice regarding grammar- and spelling-checking software is a paraphrase of a line that Richard Bach wrote long ago in his book *Jonathan Livingston Seagull*: **Judgment: Use it or lose it.**

STAGE FOUR CHECKLIST: PROOFREADING

❏ Run spelling- and grammar-checking software on the computer.

❏ Re-check spelling by reading the document yourself.

❏ Check margins for consistency.

❏ Check page numbers; be sure they are consecutive.

❏ Check format of subheads and other section markings: Are they consistent throughout the document?

❏ After printing the document, leaf through each page to be sure that

→ every page is present,

→ there are not blank sheets, and

→ all pages fed evenly into the printer.

STAGE FIVE: WIN BY LETTING GO

When you have done the best you can, send the document out and forget it. The number of consequences that can come from the document is limited, depending on the person to whom you have written:

- Your boss will either like it or hate it. Most likely, he'll like some parts, make a few changes in other parts, and leave the rest alone.
- Your client or prospective client will either like your idea and buy it, or like the idea and be unable to buy it for some reason entirely unrelated to you, or he'll find that your proposal doesn't meet his needs right now. He won't buy it, and your life will go on.
- Okay, maybe the entire civilized world will come crashing down on your head because of some error you made in composing this document, but how likely is that really?

Celebrate completion even if you did not achieve perfection. Once you've completed and sent out your work, any time you spend worrying about your reader's response is wasted. When you drop the document in the mailbox or hand it to the delivery service or press "Send," that project is over. Even if you think you will have to do another round of revisions, your initial burst of work is complete.

Get busy with something else while you wait for feedback. If you call the person to whom you wrote the letter and she says, "I received your letter but I wasn't sure what you were suggesting," you will know that you didn't deliver your message clearly. You can learn from your mistakes (and possibly save the deal) by asking, "What parts were unclear? Maybe I can explain them now." Every memo, letter, proposal, or report is a practice exercise that prepares you to express yourself a little better the next time.

The most important thing to bear in mind after sending out each document is that *you did it*. You confronted and overcame your anxieties. You made the effort to compose your ideas into words, to put those words onto paper, and to reach out to another person. Whether you did it with the desire to inform, sell, persuade, warn, deny, or anything else, you used language to help you reach out to another human being. And no matter how well or how poorly you might have expressed yourself, next time you will do better.

There is an old joke about a tourist in New York City who asks a passerby, "How do you get to Carnegie Hall?" The New Yorker answers, "Practice, practice, practice." The more you write, the better writer you will be.

ASSIGNING A WRITING PROJECT: "AS LONG AS NECESSARY, AS SOON AS POSSIBLE"

My nine-year-old daughter recently had to complete an arduous school assignment. Her teacher told her to write eight sentences about a book the class had read. It had to be eight. My daughter chewed her pencil, flounced around the house, leafed through the book, wrote two sentences, and then collapsed in tears.

"What's the matter?"

"I have to write *eight* sentences, and I only have two!"

My husband suggested that she write, "This is my first sentence about the book. This is my second sentence about the book" and so on until the homework was done. He was joking, but he had a point: If you assign a writing task in quantitative terms such as the number of words or sentences, the writer will become focused more on generating the requisite number of words than on communicating the message.

Many years ago, I worked for someone who gave me a writing assignment. I asked him how long he wanted the piece to be and by when he wanted it. "I can't tell you exactly how long it should be because I don't know all the information you're going to come up with. I need it immediately, but it won't do me any good if you rush through it and turn in something I can't use," he replied. "Make it as long necessary. Turn it in as soon as possible."

These guidelines focused my attention on the quality of the product rather than on the quantity of the words. When deciding whether to include a piece of information, I asked myself "Is this necessary?" When I felt tempted to linger over a magazine in the lunch room, I remembered that my boss needed this project as soon as possible, and I sent myself back to work. Although the directive was not specific, it was clear.

Assigning a writing project to another person is different from making a simple request like, "Get me this by Friday." You are asking the other person to engage intellectually and emotionally. It's not the same as asking a carpenter to cut lengths of wood or a manufacturer to produce a set quantity of widgets by a certain time. When asking another person to write for you:

- **Focus the writer's attention on the ultimate purpose of the document.**
- **Remind him of the main point.**
- **Urge him to consider the end-reader.**

If the ultimate recipient is you, then tell the writer what aspects of the issue are most important to you. Don't make him guess. Don't assume he already knows. If the ultimate reader is a client, a judge, a government agency, or someone else, then take a moment to talk with the writer about the needs of this particular reader.

- **Give a general idea of the length you expect, but give a range rather than an absolute number.**

Tell him you expect it to be about a page long, or three to five pages long, or around ten pages long. By assigning an approximate length, you let the writer know what you expect without triggering the urge to regress to the high-school habit of tweaking margins and font size in order to get the "right" length without considering whether he's communicated the intended information.

EDITING FOR OTHERS

No passion in the world, no love or hate, is equal to the passion to alter someone else's draft.
                    —H.G. Wells

Many business situations might cast you into the role of the editor. You may be correcting a letter or memo that an employee has written for you to sign. You may need to approve advertising or marketing copy prepared by a staff member or an outside agency. You might try to reduce your work load by delegating some of your writing tasks to others, and then find that in the time you spent editing their drafts, you could have written the whole thing yourself.

When you edit another person's work, bear in mind how you feel when someone edits *your* writing. People are often quite sensitive about their work, and they don't like being made to feel stupid or wrong—even if they are. In fact, especially if they are.

Editing for others requires tact and sensitivity—and not just because that's the nicer way to behave. Editing requires tact because the person's work will not improve if he is too intimidated to think. As the poet T.S. Eliot wrote, "An editor should tell the author his writing is better than it is. Not a lot better, a little better."

Deal with the faults of others as gently as with your own.
                    —Chinese proverb

BASIC PRINCIPLES OF EDITING FOR OTHERS

In every other section of this book, I've advised you to opt for the shorter, more "to the point" phrasing of your message. However, when you are offering criticism or feedback on someone else's writing, I suggest that you be tactful—even if that means using more words than you need. Here are a few suggestions about offering editorial suggestions to others:

USE MANY WORDS

Why should you "pad" your criticism with extra words? The extra words dull the impact of your message and therefore make the message easier to hear. If you want a person to absorb your criticism and learn from it, allow him to retain his dignity and self-respect. Soften your criticism with kind, courteous language.

BE POLITE

Criticizing sensitively often requires you to voice your message more tentatively or indirectly than you might have phrased it to yourself. In other words, you have to be tactful, sensitive, and compassionate. But don't worry that you'll turn into a cream-puff: Your kindness will help you generate a productive result. You will have a colleague or employee who will probably, over time, require less of your editorial time and energy.

BE CONSTRUCTIVE

Offer specific suggestions with each criticism. If you can't think of something to fix the problem you're noting, say so, and spend a few minutes with the writer trying to come up with several alternative solutions.

DON'T GET PERSONAL

You can't annihilate a person's self-esteem and then expect him to bounce back like a jolly little clown to do your bidding. If your goal is to have the other person become a more effective writer, focus on the *writing,* not on the writer. Compare the following examples of impersonal versus personal criticism. Which of these criticisms would *you* rather hear?

Focusing on the Principle	Focusing on the Person
"Let's put a topic sentence at the beginning of each new paragraph."	"You neglected to write a topic sentence for your paragraph."
"We are trying to use the active voice more often than the passive voice. Remember that the passive voice usually shows up in *by* phrases or with helping verbs such as *have, has,* and *had.* There are several examples of the passive voice in this document. Please go over it	"You have failed to conform to our company policy regarding use of the passive voice. Take this document back and fix it!"

again and turn those passive verbs into active ones. Thank you."

"The semicolon separates parts of a sentence that could stand alone. Do you want to change that semicolon to a comma or tinker with the sentence so that there's a short but complete sentence on each side of the semicolon?"

"You used the semicolon wrong. How do you intend to fix it?"

"The ideal average sentence length is 10 to 17 words. This sentence seems a little long. let's count the words . . . Okay. 45 words."

"This sentence is four lines long! Do you honestly think that anyone is going to read it?"

(At this point, the writer is probably thinking, "How embarrassing!" His inner critic is probably doing such a thorough job of humiliation that there is no need for you to join the chorus. Just say, "Let's look at a few ways we could shorten this sentence to break it into several shorter sentences, and still get your idea across.")

"I know how much you want this proposal to be accepted. I want that, too. That's why I think that the section on the benefits of our services should be reworked, with more focus on how we can solve the client's problems. Can you revise this section, keeping the customers' needs more in the spotlight?"

"You have spent so much space telling them how brilliant you are that you forgot to explain why they should hire us. Go over this again and get your ego out of the way!"

"Many people wonder about whether to capitalize words like federal or state in phrases like these. When federal is used as an adjective, it is not capitalized. So instead of 'According to Federal law . . . ,' you'll need to write, 'According to federal law. . . .' Could you go through this document and make the necessary changes? Thanks."

"Think about every time you've seen a reference to 'federal law' in print. Have you EVER seen it capitalized? Well, guess what. It shouldn't be capitalized here either! Take this back and correct these errors. And don't give it back to me until you have it RIGHT."

DON'T CHANGE SOMEONE'S WORK JUST FOR THE SAKE OF CHANGING

Why do we always think that we can say something better than the other person can? Sometimes it is because we really can, and sometimes it's because we've succumbed to the overwhelming urge to change another person's wording just because we didn't write it ourselves. Before you request a change, ask yourself if the change will be an improvement.

DON'T EXPECT A PERSON TO IMPROVE EVERYTHING AT ONCE

Perhaps the person whose work you are editing has problems with organizing, punctuation, using the passive voice, and belaboring his points. Work on these difficulties one at a time.

For a few documents, ask him to focus specifically on one mutually agreed upon problem area. After you see improvement in that area, select another area to work on. Little by little, you will see improvement.

END EVERY EDITING SESSION ON A POSITIVE NOTE

Even if the person did a terrible job at writing, you can compliment the effort and time that went into the attempt. Find something good to say!

EDIT E-MAIL EFFECTIVELY

Spelling errors, grammar gaffes, and fuzzy logic are careening through cyberspace at an awful rate. Even people who would ordinarily revise an important letter many times think nothing of pressing "send" to "distribution" without giving their message a second glance. Then their typos and garbled ideas pop straight into the computer terminals of their increasingly impatient colleagues all over the world. How can you avoid being the source of egregious e-mail? Read on.

Composing e-mail may not feel like writing. But it is writing, and it deserves the care you would put into any written work. The good news is that you can make your message as clear as possible before you send it. The bad news is that computer messages go everywhere instantly and then stick around forever. Many e-mailers squander the benefit of easy message transmission by zapping their stream of consciousness straight into cyberspace without pausing to revise. If you want to write excellent e-mail, follow these simple rules:

1. Re-read each e-mail message carefully before you send it.

Remember—no message is so brief that you can't make a fool of yourself by misspelling a simple word. And any message that might be read by hundreds of people deserves to be carefully crafted.

2. Use the "Subject" line to hook your reader.

The words in your "Subject" line may determine whether your message is read or deleted, so try to put the essence of your message or request into it.

3. Pare your distribution list.

It's easy for you to add another name to your "BCC" list—but not so easy for the person who receives your message to open it, read it, and figure out why on earth you sent it before pressing "delete." Cull through your distribution lists and make sure that every person is on the list for a valid reason. When people know that you have thought about whether this e-mail is appropriate for them, they will be more likely to open and read your messages.

4. When forwarding a message, delete all the gobbledygook at the top of the message.

What could make a person feel more special than to see that she is the 400th person to receive the cute message you are forwarding? A lot. Delete all previous addressees before forwarding; that way your reader can get straight into the body of the e-mail.

5. Avoid colloquialisms when writing for an international audience.

If your e-mail messages go abroad, follow the same principles that you would follow in all cross-cultural communication. Avoid cultural in-jokes, slang phrases, references to exclusively American holidays such as Thanksgiving, and other gaffes of ethnocentrism.

6. Don't mark every message "urgent."

Remember the boy who cried "wolf"? If you call everything "urgent," your colleagues will soon conclude that nothing is really urgent, except that they delete messages from you without reading them.

Part 10.

ELUDING TO YOUR DEPLORABLE ASSETS

Too caustic? To hell with the cost. If it's a good picture, we'll make it."

— Samuel Goldwyn

"I'm a master at deploring," announced the head of marketing at a high-tech startup. "My sales team can be deplorable at a moment's notice." The person who said this meant, of course, *deploying* and *deployable*. What was truly deplorable was his use of language. Nevertheless, he continued to use *deplore* instead of *deploy* throughout a two-hour business presentation. This marketing honcho made himself seem ridiculous by misusing a word. People make other embarrassingly incorrect word choices in business communications every day.

There is only one thing worse than spelling a word incorrectly, and that is *using* a word incorrectly. You can call a misspelled word a *typo*, but you can't wiggle out of a mistaken word choice. In this section, I will list some words that are frequently misused. I'll define each term very briefly and use both words in a sentence to demonstrate the difference between them. In addition to the list, I'll identify some of the most common motivations for word abuse and give you a few tips on how to figure out if you're about to condemn yourself to word-abuse hell. All of these tools will help you to be sure that your words actually mean what you think they mean.

WHY DO WE EMBARRASS OURSELVES LIKE THIS?

To know that we know what we know, and that we do not know what we do not know, that is true knowledge.
        —Lao-tzu

Writers use words incorrectly for a variety of reasons.

1. They don't know what the word means, and they don't know that they don't know.

What could be worse than to be ignorant and not to know that you are ignorant?

2. They aren't sure what the word means, and they don't care if they use it incorrectly.

Carelessness about words may be a symptom of a general attitude of carelessness about doing quality work. If you are reading this book, you are probably among the people who do care about quality and self-improvement. Watch out for people who don't share your concern for clear writing: You're likely to end up editing their work.

Why would a writer use words that he knows might be incorrect? Maybe he is in a hurry. Maybe he is writing something that will be signed by another person, so he doesn't feel the mistake will reflect on him personally. Maybe he hates his employer and unconsciously wants to make the company look bad. Or maybe he doesn't even bother to generate a rationalization. "This word or that word: what's the difference?" this person may feel, "Just let me get this piece of paper off my desk and into the mail as quickly as possible."

If you are the employer of a person who seems to have this "who cares?" attitude, let him know that you care about the way your company presents itself and that you expect him to be certain about his word choice and spelling. The attitude of not caring about the quality of his work or about the impression he is making for your firm is a serious issue. No business can afford to have employees who don't care about quality.

3. They realize that the word they're using might be wrong, but they assume that the reader will understand the basic message anyway.

The reader may indeed be able to figure out the gist of the message from the context of the document. However, he will also pick up another message: The writer either doesn't care that he's made a mistake or is suffering from the worst form of ignorance. Don't send that message about yourself.

My advice is this: Don't fake it. If you are not absolutely sure what a word means, either look it up, ask a knowledgeable person, or choose a different word. Our language is rich in words. You can find another way to convey the same idea without using a word that will betray your lack of knowledge.

4. They believe that they must use a long or technical word in order to seem intelligent.

You do not need to use long or difficult words to make yourself seem intelligent. Make your message brief and clear, and you will automatically seem smart.

WORD ABUSE PREVENTION TIPS

1. Look at the structure of the word for clues about its meaning.

Prefixes, suffixes, and word roots give you important information about a word's meaning. (An extensive list of prefixes, suffixes, and word roots appears on pages 247–55.)

2. Read many different kinds of publications, and pay attention to how words are used.

The more you read, the more confident you will be that you are using language correctly. Be sure to read publications that target the same sorts of people to whom you are writing. Read what your readers read.

3. When writing for a business audience, don't get too creative.

Innovation is a great thing, but if you're thinking of using a word in a way that it's never been used before, don't do it. Focus your innovative energies elsewhere. Let your customers and colleagues know that you are a regular person who uses appropriate language.

4. Get friendly with your local dictionary.

If you don't already own a current dictionary, go out and buy one. Then use it. Either look up the word in a real dictionary or use your computer's dictionary program.

Whatever word-processing software you are using, find out how to use it to check word definitions. In some programs, you simply highlight the word and press a certain key, and a simple definition will pop up immediately.

A SHORT LIST OF FREQUENTLY MISUSED WORDS

The definitions in this section are much simpler than those you would find in the dictionary. I have chosen only the most commonly used—and misused—meanings.

ACCEPT VERSUS EXCEPT

ACCEPT (verb) means to receive favorably or willingly.

EXCEPT (preposition or conjunction) means to leave out or exclude.

> How can I accept the fact that you are inviting everyone except me?

ADVERSE VERSUS AVERSE

ADVERSE (adjective) means antagonistic, harmful, or unfavorable.

AVERSE (adjective) means literally "turning away from." It implies a sense of being strongly disinclined or of having a feeling of opposition or distaste.

I am not averse to canceling the trip if the circumstances are adverse.

ADVISE VERSUS ADVICE

ADVISE (verb) means to inform, tell, or give notice to.

ADVICE (noun) is an opinion about what could or should be done about a situation or problem.

I advise you not to take her advice.

AFFECT VERSUS EFFECT

AFFECT (verb or noun) in its verbal usage means to act on; to produce an effect; to impress the mind or move the feelings. As a noun, it is a psychological term that describes a person's emotional state.

EFFECT (noun or verb) means result or consequence. In general, you can simplify your life by using *affect* only as a verb and using *effect* only as a noun. By following this principle, you'll minimize the likelihood of mixing up these two words.

His entire life has been affected by his inability to see the effect of his own actions.

ACCESS VERSUS EXCESS

ACCESS (noun or verb) means right of entry or admittance.

EXCESS (noun or adjective) means surplus, an amount beyond what is necessary or normal.

As soon as he turns 21, he will have access to the excess money in his trust fund.

ALLUSION VERSUS ILLUSION

ALLUSION (noun) is an indirect reference or a hint about something that is supposed to be known.

ILLUSION (noun) is an erroneous perception of reality or a false impression.

> I resent your allusion to my "wealthy lifestyle" because your perception of my wealth is an illusion.

ALTERNATE VERSUS ALTERNATIVE

ALTERNATE (noun, verb, or adjective) as a verb means to change back and forth between conditions. As an adjective, *alternate* means being in a constant state of succession or rotation, or every second one of a series. As a noun, *alternate* is the item that substitutes for another.

ALTERNATIVE (noun or adjective) in its noun form refers to a choice limited to one of two or more possibilities. It also refers to one of the things, propositions, or courses that can be chosen. As an adjective, *alternative* means affording a choice of two or more things, propositions, or courses that are mutually exclusive.

> Alternate your tires in alternate years; the alternative to good tire care is risking a blowout while you're driving.

AMOUNT VERSUS NUMBER

AMOUNT (noun or verb) refers to a sum of money or a quantity of something that is not counted in discrete units.

NUMBER (noun or verb) refers to something that can be counted in individual units.

It was an enormous amount of work to ascertain the exact number of votes received by each candidate.

ANECDOTE VERSUS ANTIDOTE

ANECDOTE (noun) is a brief story that illustrates a point.

ANTIDOTE (noun) is a substance that counteracts a poison. Don't say, "Let me share an antidote," unless you are holding a vial of anti-venom.

She told an anecdote about some children who thought that kissing a toad was an antidote for warts.

APPRAISE VERSUS APPRISE

APPRAISE (verb) means to place a value on or judge the worth of something.

APPRISE (verb) means to inform or give oral or written notice. *Apprise* is always followed by *of*.

I am writing to apprise you of my intention to appraise the property.

ASSENT VERSUS ASCENT

ASSENT (noun) means agreement.

ASCENT (noun) means an upward climb.

The Chinese government gave its assent for the team's ascent of Mount Everest.

ASSURE, ENSURE, AND INSURE

ASSURE (verb) means to state in a convincing manner so as to remove doubt.

ENSURE (verb) means to secure or make certain of.

INSURE (verb) means to guarantee against a monetary loss of (life, property, etc.) with insurance.

> I assure you that I will insure your diamond necklace before I wear it. This will ensure that if it is stolen, I will be able to replace it for you.

BESIDE VERSUS BESIDES

BESIDE is a preposition, with the original meaning "by the side of."

BESIDES may work either as a preposition or as an adverb. As a preposition, it has the sense of *in addition to,* as in *besides all this.* As an adverb, *besides* means "moreover."

> Why do I think they're romantically involved? He sat beside her at the party. Besides, I saw him kiss her ear.

My advice: Don't use *besides* at all. Use *beside* as a preposition describing something as being at the side of something else. For cases in which you are tempted to write *besides,* use *moreover, also,* or *in addition to.*

CAPITAL VERSUS CAPITOL

CAPITAL (noun) refers to a city or to a letter of the alphabet that is not lower-cased. *Capital* also refers to wealth or resources.

CAPITOL (noun) is a building where lawmakers meet.

> The residents of the state capital objected to the capital that was spent on renovating the state capitol.

CLIMACTIC VERSUS CLIMATIC

CLIMACTIC (adjective) is derived from *climax;* it refers to the point of greatest intensity in a series or progression of events.

CLIMATIC (adjective) is derived from *climate;* it refers to ongoing weather conditions.

> After the climactic explosion of Krakatoa in 1883, climatic changes were observed in many distant lands.

CITE VERSUS SITE

CITE (verb) means to quote a book or authority, to call to mind, or to give as an example. Remember the saying, He cited chapter and verse. Think of the word *citation,* which is a piece of paper that a police officer gives you when you drive too fast.

SITE (noun) has the same Latin root as the words *situation* and *situate.* It means a location, place, or geographic position (including a location on the Internet).

> In his speech, the governor cited the legislature's previous rulings about selecting sites for future landfills.

CONNOTE VERSUS DENOTE

CONNOTE (verb) means to imply, suggest indirectly, or to refer to some meaning in addition to the one explicitly stated.

DENOTE (verb) means to mean or to be a mark or sign of.

> I know that to you, "street-walking clothes" denote the clothes you would **not** wear to the gym; however, for most people, the word "street-walking" connotes prostitution.

COMPLEMENT VERSUS COMPLIMENT

COMPLEMENT (verb or noun) means to make complete or perfect.

COMPLIMENT (verb or noun) is an expression of praise.

> I must compliment you on that beautiful scarf. It complements your outfit perfectly.

COMPOSE VERSUS COMPRISE

COMPOSE (verb) means to make a whole by combining several parts.

COMPRISE (verb) means to include or contain.

> The whole comprises the parts, and the parts compose the whole.

> The United States comprises fifty states.

> Fifty states compose the United States.

CONTINUAL VERSUS CONTINUOUS

CONTINUAL (adjective) means frequently repeated.

CONTINUOUS (adjective) means without interruption.

> Your continual bickering is giving me a continuous headache.

COUNCIL VERSUS COUNSEL

COUNCIL (noun) is an administrative or governing body.

COUNSEL (noun or verb) is advice or the process of giving advice.

> The city council requested the counsel of the city engineer.

DISCREET VERSUS DISCRETE

DISCREET (adjective) means tactful, respectful of privacy, and unlikely to discuss matters of a delicate or private nature.

DISCRETE (adjective) means separate, distinct, or having several individual parts.

> The FBI had to be discreet as it gathered each discrete piece of evidence.

DISINTERESTED VERSUS UNINTERESTED

DISINTERESTED (adjective) means impartial, unbiased, and objective.

UNINTERESTED (adjective) means indifferent, having no interest.

> People who judge Olympic gymnastics competitions should be disinterested but not uninterested.

DUNGEON VERSUS DUDGEON

DUNGEON (noun) is a dark, often underground chamber or cell used to confine prisoners.

DUDGEON (noun) is a quaint term for a bad mood. This word is invariably used in the phrase *in high dudgeon* to indicate that a person is in an angry or indignant frame of mind.

> You could get thrown into a low dungeon for being in high dudgeon.

EMINENT VERSUS IMMINENT

EMINENT (adjective) means standing out above others; prominent, outstanding, or noteworthy.

IMMINENT (adjective) means likely to occur at any moment.

> This eminent institution is in imminent danger of bankruptcy.

ENVELOP VERSUS ENVELOPE

ENVELOP (verb) is to cover or surround.

ENVELOPE (noun) is a flat paper container.

> We plan to envelop each invitation in a translucent plastic envelope.

FARTHER VERSUS FURTHER

FARTHER (adverb) means a longer distance

FURTHER (adverb) means to a greater degree or extent.

> At the risk of annoying you further, I'd like to ask you how much farther we have to walk.

FEWER VERSUS LESS

FEWER (adjective) means of a smaller number. Use it when referring to something that can be counted in individual units.

LESS (adjective) refers to a smaller amount of money or degree of something that is not counted in discrete units.

> The fewer responsibilities you have, the less likely you are to succeed.

FLAUNT VERSUS FLOUT

FLAUNT (verb) is to make a brazen or gaudy display.

FLOUT (verb) is to scoff at or defy with open contempt.

You don't have to flaunt the fact that you are flouting the law.

FOREWORD VERSUS FORWARD

FOREWORD (noun) is a brief introduction at the beginning of a book. *Fore* as in before, *word* as in word. A foreword is a word (or two) that comes before.

FORWARD is an adverb that refers to something just ahead or something that one is moving toward.

Now that I have finished reading the foreword, I am looking forward to reading the book.

FLOUNDER VERSUS FOUNDER

FLOUNDER (noun) is a kind of fish. As a verb, *flounder* means to struggle helplessly.

FOUNDER (verb) is to fail or collapse.

FOUNDER (noun) is the person who originates an organization or social movement.

The founder's floundering flounder restaurant has finally foundered.

HISTORIC VERSUS HISTORICAL

HISTORIC (adjective) refers to an event of great and lasting importance.

HISTORICAL (adjective) refers to any occurrence in the distant past.

Every historical event is not necessarily historic.

IMPLY VERSUS INFER

IMPLY (verb) means to indicate or suggest without stating explicitly.

INFER (verb) means to derive by reasoning, to conclude or judge from premises or evidence.

The person who is sending the communication does the *implying;* the person who is getting the communication must *infer* or deduce the meaning of what the sender implied.

I am implying that you inferred incorrectly.

INCREDIBLE VERSUS INCREDULOUS

INCREDIBLE (adjective) means hard to believe or seemingly impossible.

INCREDULOUS (adjective) means skeptical or indicating disbelief.

I find it incredible that he was incredulous about something so obvious.

LIE VERSUS LAY

LIE (verb or noun) means to recline or rest on a surface. This verb does not take an object. You lie on the bed, lie down, or you are lying down. *Lie* (verb or noun) also means an untruth or a false statement.

LAY (verb) means to put or place something on a surface. Lay must be followed by an object, such as in *lay the book down* or *chickens lay eggs*.

The past tense of *lie* is *lay.* This is tricky: the present tense of *lay* is *lay,* as in he told me to *lie down,* and I *lay down.* But he told me to *lay it down,* and I *laid it down.*

She lays out her clothes for the next day every night before she lies down to sleep.

LOATH VERSUS LOATHE

LOATH (adjective) means unwilling, reluctant, or disinclined.

LOATHE (verb) describes a feeling of intense revulsion or disgust.

I am loath to visit these people whom I loathe.

LOSE VERSUS LOOSE

You know what LOSE (verb) means. It is the opposite of *find or gain.*

You know what LOOSE (adjective) means, too. It is the opposite of tight. So why have I included this word pair on this list? Because I have received writing samples containing sentences like "If we loose this account we may have difficulty meeting our sales quotas for the next quarter."

Your loose speech may lead you to lose your job.

MANTEL VERSUS MANTLE

MANTEL (noun) is a shelf that provides a place for you to put your family pictures and little art objects.

MANTLE (noun) is a cloak or coat.

He tried several times to put his mantle on the mantel, but it kept slipping off.

PEAK VERSUS PEEK VERSUS PIQUE

PEAK (noun) is a pinnacle, the highest point of a mountain or a career.

PEEK (verb) means to steal a glance at something that you were not supposed to look at. *Peek* can be either a noun or a verb.

PIQUE (verb or noun) comes from the French word meaning *to pick or goad.* It means to stimulate a person's feelings sharply, usually in an irritating manner.

> He was piqued by the fact that she had peeked at the peak before he reached the summit.

PERSONAL VERSUS PERSONNEL

PERSONAL (adjective) refers to something private, intimate, or having to do with a particular person.

PERSONNEL (noun) is a general term referring to the employees of a company. The term *personnel* is meant to distinguish between the human resources of a firm and its *material* or physical resources.

> Please do not make personal remarks to our personnel.

PERSPECTIVE VERSUS PROSPECTIVE

To have or to use PERSPECTIVE (noun) means to view or depict all the elements of a scene in a way that shows an understanding of their inter-relationships.

PROSPECTIVE (adjective) means likely to happen in the future.

> When a prospective employer promises that its stock options are sure to triple in value, be sure to view that promise from the perspective of recent economic history.

PRECEDE VERSUS PROCEED

PRECEDE (verb) means to go before. The prefix *pre-* tells you that this word must refer to something that happened earlier (think of *preview*).

PROCEED (verb) means to go forward or continue. The prefix *pro-* gives the word its sense of forward movement (think of *propel*).

PROCEEDS, when used as a noun, means the funds that are generated from a sale or transaction.

> Planning precedes the choice of venue. After choosing the venue, we can proceed to the selection of caterers and entertainment. Naturally, all proceeds of the event will be donated to charity.

PREMIER VERSUS PREMIERE

PREMIER (adjective) describes something that is first in rank or quality.

PREMIERE (noun) designates the first time a new work is performed or shown in public.

> The success of the movie's premiere proved that the film's director is one of the premier film-makers working today.

PRINCIPAL VERSUS PRINCIPLE

PRINCIPAL (noun or adjective) sometimes refers to the main body of an estate, as distinguished from the interest one earns from that asset. *Principal* also refers to the person whose office you get sent to when you misbehave in elementary school. It can also refer to the prima ballerina in a ballet or to the star of a theatrical production. As an adjective, *principal* means first or highest in rank, importance, or value. It can also pertain to one's invested capital.

PRINCIPLE (noun) is an accepted or professed rule of action or conduct; a fundamental, primary, or general law or truth from which others are derived; a fundamental doctrine or tenet.

> I learned two important principles as a child: Always cover your mouth when you sneeze, and never spend your principal.

RISE VERSUS RAISE

RISE (verb or noun) means to move from a lower to a higher position or to ascend. This word does not take an object. You might rise *from* bed in the morning, but you do not rise the bed. *Rise* also means to increase in number, amount, or value.

RAISE (verb or noun) means to elevate or pick something up, to cause to rise up. Like *lay*, *raise* must be followed by an object, such as in *raise your hand.*

> Please rise, come to the front of the courtroom, and raise your right hand.

> He's decided to raise cotton because he thinks that prices for natural fabrics are sure to rise.

SIT VERSUS SET

SIT (verb) means to be seated, located, or situated.

SET (verb) means to put or place in a specified position.

> Please set your briefcase on the table and sit down so that we can talk.

STATIONERY VERSUS STATIONARY

STATIONERY (noun) refers to writing paper and envelopes.

STATIONARY (adjective) means standing still.

> A stationary bike is one that does not roll. A stationery bike would be a bike that is made out of writing paper.

TAUNT VERSUS TAUT

TAUNT (verb) means to tease in a mocking, insulting, or contemptuous manner.

TAUT (adjective) means pulled or drawn tight. *Taut* is the opposite of slack.

> Don't taunt her because her abdominal muscles aren't taut!

TENANT VERSUS TENET

TENANT (noun) is one who pays rent to use or occupy land, a building, or property owned by another.

TENET (noun) is a principle, belief, or doctrine that a person or organization holds or maintains as true.

> It is a basic tenet of property management that the tenant must pay rent.

THEN VERSUS THAN

THEN (adverb) means at that time or soon afterward. Sometimes it introduces a logical consequence, as in the pattern *If . . . , then . . .*

THAN (conjunction or adverb) is a word that helps differentiate between two elements in a comparison.

If you arrive at the airport later than 9:00, then you will surely miss the plane.

THREW VERSUS THROUGH

THREW (verb) is the past tense of the verb *to throw*.

THROUGH is a preposition indicating that something passed in the midst of something else.

She threw the baseball through the window.

THRU is a barbarism that does not even merit being called a word. Do not use it in any business communications.

This list covers just a few of the sets of words that are mangled and misused every day. Search the Internet under "commonly confused words" and you'll find dozens more. Information about the meaning, usage, and spelling of words is easily available—if you seek it out.

Using precise, colorful words will enrich your writing, but only if you use them correctly. If you don't want to spend the time to confirm the meaning of a word, then limit your vocabulary to words of whose meaning you are certain.

I implore you: Use a plain, simple word correctly rather than humiliating yourself by using a term incorrectly. If you're not absolutely sure what a word means, either look it up or use a different term. You will come to regret it if you send off a letter about *eluding to the past* or some other such gaffe.

INTERNET RESOURCES FOR WRITERS

Enormous resources are available to you on the Internet. Here are just a few of the excellent sites for information on grammar, word choice, and other writing-related issues. See the Bibliography for a list of resource books.

http://www.yourDictionary.com

http://www.dictionary.com

http://www.sec.gov/news/handbook.htm (Plain English Handbook compiled by the Securities and Exchange Commission)

http://www.educast.com.sg/home/englishinahurry.htm

http://www.useit.com/papers/webwriting (Writing for the Web)

http://www.telp.com/editing/sfindex.htm (Frequently Asked Questions about Copy Editing)

BIBLIOGRAPHY

For a complete bibliography of references used in writing *Get to the Point!*, go to *www.worktalk.com* and click on "Get to the Point." The site also features new ideas and writing resources, as well as information about Worktalk's on-site and on-line writing trainings.

PREFIXES, SUFFIXES, AND WORD ROOTS

When you understand the logic behind a word and can see what the word is made of, you will understand it better. And use it better. And understand the nuance and connotation better. You will just be a better writer in every way if you learn to dissect words. Since English contains so many words that come to us through Greek and Latin, a basic knowledge of Greek and Latin roots, prefixes, and suffixes will help you enormously. Here is a collection of the most commonly used Greek and Latin root words, prefixes, and suffixes.

BASE	MEANING	ORIGIN
act	to act	Latin
acu, acr, ac	needle	Latin
alt	high	Latin
anima, anim	life, mind	Latin
ann, enn	year	Latin
anthrop	man	Greek
aqua	water	Latin
arch, archi	govern, rule	Greek
arm	army, weapon	Latin
arbitr, arbiter	to judge, consider	Latin
art	craft, skill	Latin
arthr, art	segment, joint	Greek
aud	to hear	Latin
bell	war	Latin
biblio, bibl	book	Greek
bio	life	Greek
capit, cipit	head	Latin

caus	cause, case, lawsuit	Latin
cede	to go, yield	Latin
cele	honor	Latin
cell	to rise, project	Latin
cent	one hundred	Latin
cept, capt, cip, cap, ceive, ceipt	to take, hold, grasp	Latin
cert	sure, to trust	Latin
cess, ced	to move, withdraw	Latin
cid, cis	to cut off, be brief, to kill	Latin
circ, circum	around	Latin
civ	citizen	Latin
claud	close, shut, block	Latin
clin	to lean, lie, bend	Latin
cog	to know	Latin
column	a column	Latin
comput	to compute	Latin
cont	to join, unite	Latin
cor, cord, cour, card	heart	Latin
corp	body	Latin
cosm	world, order, universe	Greek
crac, crat	rule, govern	Greek
cred	believe, trust	Latin
crit, cris	separate, discern, judge	Latin

culp	fault, blame	Latin
curs, curr, corr	to run	Latin
custom	one's own	Latin
dem	people	Greek
dent, odon	tooth	Latin
derm	skin	Greek
dic, dict	to say, to speak, assert	Latin
duct, duc	to lead, draw	Latin
dur	to harden, hold out	Latin

PREFIX LIST

BASE	MEANING	ORIGIN
ab-	away	Latin
acro-	top, tip, end	Greek
ad-, ac-, at-, as-, ap-, am-, an-, ar-, ag-, af-	to, toward, at	Latin
ambi-	around, both	Latin
amphi-	both, of both sides, around	Greek
ant-, anti-	against	Greek
ante-	before	Latin
apo-, ap-, aph-	away from, off	Greek
archa-, arshae-	old, ancient	Greek
auto-	self	Greek
ben-, bon-	good, well	Latin

bi-	two	Latin
co-, con-, com-	together, with	Latin
contra-, contro-	against	Latin
de-	from, away, off	Latin
deca-, dec-, deka-	ten	Greek
di-, dis-	two, twice	Greek
dia-	through, across	Greek
dis-, dif-	apart, away, not, to deprive	Latin
du-	double, two	Latin
dys-	difficult, bad	Greek
e-, ex-, ec-	out, beyond, from, out of, forth	Latin
ecto-	outside of	Greek
en-	in give [intensifier]	Latin
endo-, ento-	within	Greek
ep-, epi-	upon, at, in addition	Greek
eu-	good, well	Greek
extra-	beyond	Latin
fore-	before	Anglo-Saxon
hemi-	half	Greek
hetero-	various, unlike	Greek
hier-	sacred	Greek
holo-	whole	Greek

homo-	same	Greek
hyper-	above, beyond	Greek
hypo-, hyp-	under, less than	Greek
ideo-, idea-	idea	Greek
in-, ir-, im-, il-	not, without	Latin
in-, im-	in, on, upon, into, toward	Latin
inter-	between	Latin
intro-	within	Latin
iso-	equal	Greek
kilo-	thousand	Greek
macro-	long, large	Greek
magn-, mag-, meg-, maj-	great	Latin
mal-	bad, ill	Latin
mega-	great	Greek
met-, meta-, meth-	among, with, after, beyond	Greek
micro-	small	Greek
migr-	to move, travel	Latin
mill-	thousand	Latin
mis-	less, wrong	Latin
mono-	one	Greek
multi-	many, much	Latin
neo-	new	Greek

non-, ne-	not	Latin
o-, ob-, oc-, of-, op-	against, toward	Latin
omni-	all	Latin
paleo-	long ago, ancient	Greek
pan-, panto-	all, every	Greek
para-	beside, beyond	Latin
penta-	five	Greek
per-	through	Latin
peri-	around, about	Greek
pre-	before	Latin
pro-	before, forward, forth	Latin
pronto-	first	Greek
poly-	many	Greek
post-	after	Latin
pseudo-	false, counterfeit	Greek
quad-, quatr-	four	Latin
re-	again, anew, back	Latin
retro-	back, backward, behind	Latin
se-, sed-	apart, aside, away	Latin
semi-	half	Latin
sover-	above, over	Latin
sub-	under, below, up from below	Latin
super-, supra-	above, down, thoroughly	Latin

syn-, sym-, syl-	together, with	Greek
tele-	far off	Greek
trans-	over, across	Latin
tri-	three	Latin
un-	not	Latin
uni-	one	Latin

SUFFIX LIST

NOUN-FORMING SUFFIXES

SUFFIX	MEANING	ORIGIN
-age	belongs to	Latin
-ance	state of being	Latin
-ant	thing or one who	Latin
-ar, -ary	relating to, like	Latin
-ence	state, fact, quality	Latin
-ent	to form	Latin
-ic	like, having the nature	Latin & Greek
-ine	nature of, feminine ending	Latin
-ion, -tion, -ation	being, the result of	Latin
-ism	act, condition	Latin & Greek
-ist	one who	Latin
-ive	of, belonging to, quality of	Latin

-ment	a means, product, act, state	Latin
-or	person or thing that	Latin
-ory	place for	Latin
-ty	condition of, quality of	Latin
-y	creates abstract noun	Greek & Anglo-Saxon

ADJECTIVE-FORMING SUFFIXES

SUFFIX	MEANING	ORIGIN
-able	capable of being	Latin
-al	like, suitable for	Latin
-ance	state of being	Latin
-ant	thing or one who	Latin
-ar, -ary	relating to, like	Latin
-ate	to become associated with	Latin
-ent	to form	Latin
-ial	function of	Latin
-ible	capable of being	Latin
-ic	like, having the nature of	Latin & Greek
-ine	nature of, feminine ending	Latin
-ive	of, belonging to, quality of	Latin
-ory	place for	Latin
-ous	characterized by, having quality of	Latin

-y	quality, somewhat like	Greek & Anglo-Saxon

VERB-FORMING SUFFIXES

SUFFIX	MEANING	ORIGIN
-ate	to become associated with	Latin
-fy	make, do	Latin
-ise, -ize	to become like	Latin

ADVERB-FORMING SUFFIXES

SUFFIX	MEANING	ORIGIN
-ic	like, having the nature of	Latin & Greek
-ly	like, to extent of	Latin

INDEX